Chris Campe

TOLLERORT

Hamburgs beste Läden & Adressen
Hamburg's best shops & spots

JUNIUS

ACH, WIE TOLL!

Abends mit der U3 Richtung Hafen, an den Landungsbrücken raus, dann rauf aufs Deck der Hafenfähre und mit den Ohren im Wind der Sonne entgegen. Kein Zweifel — Hamburg ist ein toller Ort.

Wenn man mit der Fähre 62 Richtung Elbstrand fährt, zieht „Tollerort", das Original, links am anderen Elbufer vorbei. Aber auch wenn sich der Name vielversprechend anhört, die Kaizunge mit Containerterminal ist in Wirklichkeit kein *so* toller Ort, sondern nur ein ehemaliger „Zollort" im Freihafen, auf Plattdeutsch.

Alstermichelelbe — was ist denn nun wirklich toll an Hamburg? Toll sind einzigartige Cafés, die mit Leidenschaft betrieben werden; eigenwillige Läden, die es so vielleicht nur in Hamburg gibt; Fachgeschäfte alter Schule, deren Inhaber sich so sehr auf ihr Ding konzentrieren, dass sie neben ihrer Geschäftsadresse nicht mal eine Internetadresse haben; und die vielen grünen Ecken mit Aussicht.

Die ganz bekannten tollen Orte sind außen vor geblieben, denn wenn man zum Beispiel im Schanzenviertel einmal um den Pudding läuft, findet man — je nach Geschmack — die guten Läden dort auch von selbst. Berühmte Lieblinge wie der Alte Elbtunnel und die Strandperle sind aber doch dabei, denn sie *sind* einfach tolle Orte. Die übrigen zwei hundert Tipps sind so gegensätzlich wie Hamburg selbst: Die Rote Flora ist vertreten, aber auch die Elbphilharmonie, der Umsonstladen ebenso wie das Geschäft für Wohnaccessoires, der ehrwürdige Fachhändler genauso wie der Concept Store.

Toller Ort richtet sich nicht nur an Hamburg-Besucher, die gezielt mehr sehen wollen als die Landungsbrücken und den Jungfernstieg, sondern auch an Neu-Hamburgerinnen auf Entdeckungstour. Und

Alteingesessene erinnert die Sammlung an die tollen Orte, die sie zwar kennen, aber schon fast vergessen hatten, und an die, die unentdeckt etwas abseits ihrer Alltagspfade liegen.

In den zehn Abschnitten des Buchs sind jeweils mehrere Stadtteile zusammengefasst, die Einträge sind allerdings nicht streng nach Bezirken geordnet. Mithilfe der Nummern bei den Texten lassen sich die tollen Orte in den Stadtteilkarten wiederfinden, und in den beiden Registern hinten im Buch kann man gezielt suchen, im Alphabet oder nach Rubriken.

Toller Ort wurde im Sommer recherchiert und geschrieben, daher die zahlreichen Hinweise auf schöne Sonnenplätze. Die Rubrik „Drinnebleiben" im Index hinten gibt aber auch Tipps für das sprichwörtliche Hamburger Schietwetter.

Viel Spaß!

HOW GREAT!

Evenings riding the U3 U-Bahn line, destination harbor. Out to the Landungsbrücken pier, then on the deck of the harbor ferry, the wind at your back, cruising toward the sunset. No doubt about it—Hamburg is a "toller Ort," what simply means "great place" in German.

If you take ferry line 62 towards the Elbstrand beach, you'll sail by "Tollerort," the original one, the peninsula and pier to the left on the opposite shore of the Elbe River. But even though its name also translates as "great place," this pier with container terminal is actually not really that nice. It is just a former "Zollort" as they say in Low German, meaning a place to collect tolls, which at some point morphed into "Tollerort".

The Alster, the Elbe, Saint Michael's—what's really great about Hamburg? For one, its unique cafés, operated with a passion by their owners. Or the quirky only-in-Hamburg stores. Businesses run by old-school characters so fixated on their shops that their only address is bricks and mortar and no mention of a website. And of course, the city is full of patches of greenery, view included.

Most of the popular great places have been skipped over. You only need walk around the hub of the Schanze district to find the best addresses for whatever you're into. But famous old favorites such as the Elbe Tunnel and the Strandperle are listed because they simply are great places. The some two-hundred-plus tips here are as incongruous as Hamburg itself: the Rote Flora is listed, but so is the Elbe Philharmonic Hall, the give-away store, the home accessories store, the traditional specialty shop and the concept store.

Toller Ort is not only for Hamburg visitors who want to see more than just the Landungsbrücken piers and the Jungfernstieg promenade. It is also for new Hamburg residents who want to discover the city. And all these great places here can prod long-time residents into remembering things they already know but had nearly forgotten. And also show them a few undiscovered places off their usual beaten path.

Each of the book's ten sections covers several neighborhoods, but the entries are not strictly organized by city districts. The numbers next to the texts help you locate the great places on the city area maps. And the two indexes in back of the book let you find places alphabetically or by category.

Toller Ort was written during the summer, which is why it often mentions great places for enjoying sunny weather. The category "Insider" in the index offers tips for the city's proverbial "Schietwetter," what in German slang, nicely put, means crappy weather.

Have fun!

ÜBERBLICK

Tolle Orte auf den Karten

 Toller Ort   Toller Ort außerhalb der Karte   Buchladen

AUF ST. PAULI UND AM HAFEN

Pizza Bande
Lincolnstraße 10, 20359 St. Pauli

In einem toten Winkel des Kiez macht die Pizza Bande die „beste Pizza Hamburgs". Das ist zwar eine nicht weiter belegte Eigenwerbung, aber es scheint doch etwas dran zu sein, denn meistens ist der Laden rappelvoll. Nicht nur Liebhaber von Quattro Formaggi werden an der Vielfalt der Beläge zum Selbstzusammenstellen ihre Freude haben, auch die tolle Auswahl für Veganer ist hier eine Selbstverständlichkeit.

On a quiet side street off the buzzing party strip, Pizza Bande purports to make "Hamburg's best pizza." Of course that's an unsubstantiated marketing claim, but there seems to be some truth to it, because the shop is usually full to brimming. The wide variety of toppings will not only please aficionados of quattro formaggi, but will also leave vegans spoiled for choice. **pizza-bande.de**

Café Mimosa
Clemens-Schultz-Straße 87, 20359 St. Pauli

Das Mimosa ist berühmt für seine hausgemachten, fluffigen Brioches, die dort noch warm serviert werden, begleitet wahlweise von ebenfalls hausgemachter Marmelade oder – noch viel besser – Zitronensorbet oder Holundergranita. Aber auch die Paninis sind gekonnt zusammengestellt (Ziegenkäse, Honig, Traube und Rosmarin – lecker!), der Kaffee ist stark und man sitzt gemütlich unter alten St.-Pauli-Stuckdecken.

The Mimosa is famous for its homemade, fluffy brioche, served warm with a choice of jam (also homemade) or even better, with lemon sorbet or elderberry granita. But the paninis are also a real treat, with goat's cheese, honey, grapes and rosemary—divine! The coffee is good and the atmosphere relaxing under the historic ornate ceilings typical of St. Pauli. **cafemimosa.de**

3

Man muss die Landungsbrücken ganz, ganz weit hinuntergehen und eisern unzählige Fischimbisse hinter sich lassen, um am Ende der Pontons zur Fischbrötchenbude Brücke 10 zu gelangen. Dort sind die köstlichen Krabbenbrötchen so maßlos belegt, dass die Brötchendeckel im Neunzig-Grad-Winkel hochstehen. Im Angebot: zwei Nordseekrabbenbrötchen mit einer Flasche Schampus — man gönnt sich ja sonst nichts.

To get to Brücke 10, you first have to steel yourself to walk past scores of fish snack bars, eyes straight ahead. Eventually you get to the end of the pier and to Brücke 10 where you can indulge in a delicious crab sandwich piled so high that the roll can hardly hold it all together. Special offer: two North Sea crab sandwiches with a split of sparkling wine—who could ask for more. **bruecke-10.de**

4

Die osteuropäische Küche ist an diesem Ende der Elbe nicht gerade weit verbreitet, vielleicht ist das kleine Restaurant Kuchnia deswegen so beliebt und immer gut besucht. Mal was Besonderes — in Form von Borschtsch, Kraut-Moosbeere-Salat und Pierogi. Auf Wunsch begleiten Wodka-basierte Cocktails mit fantasievollen Namen die Gerichte, die mal mehr, mal weniger weiterentwickelte Varianten ihrer klassischen Vorbilder sind, aber immer lecker.

This side of the Elbe does not see too much Eastern European cuisine. Maybe that's why the little Kuchnia restaurant is so popular and always draws a crowd. Special dishes include Borscht, cabbage-cranberry salad and Pierogis. And to wash it down, try a vodka cocktail inspired by the classics but with an original twist and a poetic name. **kuchnia-wodkabar.de**

Heiligengeistfeld, mit und ohne Dom
Feldstraße, 20359 St. Pauli

Dreimal im Jahr blinken die Buden beim Hamburger Dom, der eben schon lange keine Kirche mehr ist, sondern ganz im Gegenteil „das größte Volksfest des Nordens". Mit etwas Glück ist die betonierte Fläche des Heiligengeistfelds aber gerade leer, und dann kann man von der Fußgängerbrücke aus die Sonne hinter Millerntor-Stadion und Hochbunker versinken sehen. Wo hat man das schon, so ein weites Feld mitten in der Stadt.

Three times a year, the lights are aglitter at the Hamburger Dom, which means cathedral in German, even though this spacious square hasn't seen a church for a long time. Meanwhile, the name refers to the "largest Volksfest of the North." But if you are lucky, the concrete stretches of the Heiligengeistfeld might be empty and you can watch the sunset behind the Millerntor-Stadium and the bunker from the pedestrian bridge. Where else can you find such a wide-open space in the middle of the city?

B-Movie
Brigittenstraße 5, 20359 St. Pauli

Das Team des B-Movie präsentiert in seinem ehrenamtlich und nicht-kommerziell betriebenen Programmkino sorgfältig zusammengestellte thematische Filme, Filmreihen und Veranstaltungen, die man sonst selten zu sehen bekommt. Die Filme schaut man m gemütlichen Hinterhofkino in Wohnzimmeratmosphäre, werbefrei und zu ausgesprochen günstigen Eintrittspreisen.

B-Movie is a volunteer-run, non-commercial cinema that offers a creative selection of films, film series and events rarely seen elsewhere. The films are screened in a cinema that feels like a living room, tucked away in one of Hamburg's inner courtyards, with no commercials and at a great price. b-movie.de

7

Die Zuckermonarchie erstreckt sich über viele Kämmerchen auf mehreren Etagen und sieht aus, wie man sich das Headquarter von Instagram vorstellt: alles ganz weiß und hell und vintage-chic, mit goldenen Lampen und Papier-PomPoms in Rosa. Aber die Patisserie und das Frühstück sind nicht nur Foodporn, sondern wirklich köstlich und einer Monarchie durchaus würdig.

Zuckermonarchie, or "sugar monarchy," stretches over several floors and looks like how one might imagine the headquarters of Instagram: all white and bright and vintage chic, with golden lights and pink paper pom poms. The pastries and breakfasts are more than mere food porn, however; they are truly delicious and befitting of royalty. **zuckermonarchie.de**

8

Bevor Comics als Graphic Novels wiedergeboren wurden, kannte sich in den meisten Buchhandlungen kaum jemand so richtig damit aus, und in den Comicläden gingen die künstlerischen Independent-Comics vor lauter Superhelden oft unter. Seit 2010 aber kristallisiert sich das Hamburger Comicgeschehen bei Strips & Stories. Hier gibt es eine tolle, internationale Auswahl an Graphic Novels, und die Zeichnerszene trifft sich bei Releasepartys.

Before comic strips were reborn as graphic novels, none of the book stores really knew much about the genre. And in the regular comic shops, most artistic indie comics got lost among the super heroes. But since 2010, Strips & Stories has been the vanguard of the Hamburg comics scene. The store offers a great international selection of graphic novels with events and release parties that make it a meet-up for the city's illustrator community. **strips-stories.de**

Deniz Imbiss
Talstraße 27, 20359 St. Pauli

Eine richtige Kieztour ist erst zu Ende, wenn man auf dem Nachhauseweg noch schön eine Pide bei Deniz gegessen hat. Der Imbiss in der Talstraße liegt direkt auf dem Weg und hat die ganze Nacht geöffnet, die Mitarbeiter stellen den Betrunkenen schmerzbefreit ihre letzte Mahlzeit vor Bett oder Kloschüssel bereit.

A real tour of the St. Pauli "Kiez" is only complete when you've sampled a pita sandwich from Deniz after a night on the town. The Talstrasse street snack bar is hard to miss and stays open all night. The staff make it easy for all drunks and the slightly tipsy to get one last meal before bedtime. Or worst-case scenario, a trip to the bathroom.

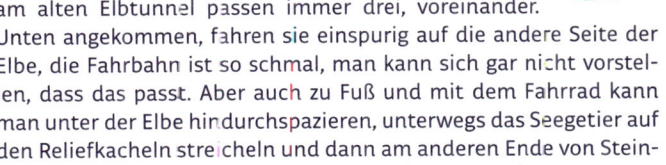

Alter Elbtunnel
Bei den St. Pauli-Landungsbrücken 5, 20359 St. Pauli

Verrückt — es gibt Aufzüge für Autos! In die Fahrkörbe am alten Elbtunnel passen immer drei, voreinander. Unten angekommen, fahren sie einspurig auf die andere Seite der Elbe, die Fahrbahn ist so schmal, man kann sich gar nicht vorstellen, dass das passt. Aber auch zu Fuß und mit dem Fahrrad kann man unter der Elbe hindurchspazieren, unterwegs das Seegetier auf den Reliefkacheln streicheln und dann am anderen Ende von Steinwerder aus die ganze Stadt sehen, wie auf einer Postkarte.

Incredible! There's even a car elevator! The lifts at the old Elbe Tunnel can fit up to three vehicles in a row. Once down below, the cars drive single file to the other shore of the Elbe River. The lane is so small that it is hard to imagine how the cars even fit. But you can also walk or bike the tunnel, stopping along the way to admire the sea creature ceramic tiles. Up on the other side in Steinwerder awaits an impressive postcard view of the city.

hamburg.de/alter-elbtunnel

Beschaulich zieht das ganz alltägliche Leben auf St. Pauli am Kraweel vorbei. Die einen gehen mal eben nebenan zu Edeka, die anderen kommen von der Schanze und sind unterwegs zum Kiez und zum Hafen. Man sitzt gemütlich bei Kaffee und Kuchen unter der Markise, mittendrin und ein Teil davon — auch wenn man vorher noch nie auf St. Pauli war.

Café Kraweel is witness to the daily ebb and flow of life in St. Pauli, with some folks popping into the adjacent Edeka grocery store and others on their way from the Schanze to the Kiez club district and the harbor. Sitting under the awning with a coffee and a piece of cake, even first-time visitors to St. Pauli feel right in the thick of things and a part of the parade of humanity. **kraweel.com**

Bestellt man am langen Tresen der Walrus Bar unbedarft einen Drink — „irgendwas mit Wodka" — und beobachtet die Barkeeper dann bei der Zubereitung, ist man erst mal skeptisch. Ist das nicht doch ein ziemlich übertriebenes Getue? Aber schon der erste Schluck überzeugt: All die esoterisch wirkenden Gesten waren wohl zweifellos nötig, um so etwas Komplexes und Gutes zu servieren.

If you order a drink at the very long bar at the Walrus Bar—"something with vodka"—and proceed to watch the bartenders make it, you may be a bit skeptical at first. It does seem like an awful lot of fuss, but one sip and you will be a convert: all those inscrutable moves were doubtless critical in serving up something so complex and tasty. **thewalrusbar.de**

Boutique Bizarre
Reeperbahn 35, 20359 St. Pauli

Die Boutique Bizarre ist sozusagen das MacBook unter den Sexshops – groß und aufgeräumt, weiß und designy. Ein Fachgeschäft für Ästheten, aber auch für Anfänger, denn der große Laden präsentiert sich ungewöhnlich offenherzig und einladender als viele seiner spelunkigeren Mitbewerber. Den eher klassischen Teil des Angebots kann man schon von der Straße aus sehen, aber nicht die Kunst-Galerie, die Fetisch- und Dessous-Abteilungen und die Latex-Sperrzone im Untergeschoss.

The Boutique Bizarre is the MacBook among sex shops— spacious, clean, white and good design. A specialty shop for connoisseurs, but novices will also feel welcome in this big store with an open attitude, unlike the dark and dingy competitors. The store windows already showcase the boutique's more conventional range. But you have to go inside to see the art gallery, the fetish and lingerie department and the restricted-access latex zone in the basement.

boutique-bizarre.de

Gartendeck
Große Freiheit 62–68, 20359 St. Pauli

Wenn man in Hamburg „Große Freiheit" hört, denkt man vielleicht nicht als erstes an Kräuterbeete und Gemüseanbau. Und doch: Auf dem Flachdach einer Parkgarage wachsen Bohnen in Bäckereikisten, Minze in Milchkartons, Tomatenpflanzen in Plastiksäcken. Alle sind willkommen, sich beim Gärtnern auf dem 1100 Quadratmeter großen Gartendeck die Hände schmutzig zu machen und urban gardening live zu erleben. Was die Gemeinschaftsbeete des temporären Gartens hergeben, wird anschließend gemeinsam verkocht und gegessen.

Hamburg's Große Freiheit street does not necessarily conjure up herb gardens and vegetable beds. But there it is—up on the flat roof of a parking garage, beans ripening in bread crates, mint in milk cartons, tomatoes in grow bags. Everyone is invited to experience urban gardening first-hand on the 1,100-square-meter Gartendeck and get some dirt under their fingernails. Members and guests often get together to cook and dine on the harvest of this temporary garden. **gartendeck.de**

HVV-Hafenfähren
Bei den St. Pauli-Landungsbrücken, 20354 St. Pauli

Ja, man kann sich von einem der falschen Kapitäne, die an den Landungsbrücken ihre Dienste feilbieten, an Bord ziehen lassen und über zwanzig Euro für eine Hafenrundfahrt bezahlen, die im Durchschnitt den Informationsgehalt und Unterhaltungswert einer Bildzeitung hat. Oder man fährt zum Preis eines Einzelfahrscheins mit der HVV-Fähre 62 die Elbe runter – an St. Pauli und am Fischmarkt vorbei, an Docks und Containerterminals, direkt zum Elbstrand in Övelgönne.

Sure, you can let one of the fast-talking captains on the St. Pauli-Landungsbrücken piers convince you to board his boat and pay twenty euros for a cruise around the harbor. Be warned: the entertainment and informational value are usually on par with Germany's beloved but trashy Bild newspaper. Or you can take HVV Ferry route 62, cruise down the Elbe, past St. Pauli and the Fish Market, around the docks and container terminals with your final destination at the Elbstrand beach in Övelgönne—all for the price of a one-way ticket on the public transit system. **hadag.de/hafenfaehren.php**

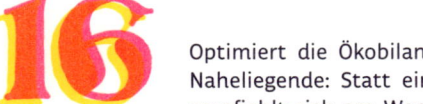

Stattreisen
Kuhberg 2, 20459 St. Pauli

Optimiert die Ökobilanz und schärft den Blick fürs Naheliegende: Statt eines Kurztrips in ferne Städte empfiehlt sich am Wochenende eine geführte Stattreisen-Tour vor der eigenen Haustür. Dass dabei auch Dinge Thema sind, die die traditionelle Heimatkunde nicht interessieren, deutet der Name des Veranstalters schon an. Wer also historisch und kritisch einordnen möchte, was in seiner unmittelbaren Umgebung geschieht, wird dabei von den Kunsthistorikern und Historikern, Architekten und Stadtplanern des Stattreisen-Teams kundig geleitet.

Protect the environment and raise awareness for what is close at hand: why not take a guided Stattreisen tour down your street this weekend rather than a short trip to a far-away city. The name of the tour company already makes clear that this is no ho-hum, traditional tour operator. Stattreisen loosely translates as alternative travel but is also a pun on the German word "Stadt" for city. So if you want a historical explanation with social critique about what is happening in your immediate vicinity, Stattreisen's team of art historians and historians, architects and urban planners will knowledgeably set you straight. **stattreisen-hamburg.de**

Kandie Shop
Wohlwillstraße 16, 20359 St. Pauli

17

Der untere Abschnitt der Wohlwillstraße mit den Wohnprojekt-Terrassenhäusern der Jägerpassage hat seinen ganz eigenen Charakter, und das Herzstück bildet der Kandie Shop zusammen mit dem Café Stark, Strips & Stories und den Jungs von Suicycle. Man sitzt gemütlich und nachbarschaftlich bei Fair-trade-Kaffee und hausgemachtem Carrot Cake – wann immer das Wetter es zulässt, draußen auf den Bänken an der Straße.

A special atmosphere prevails in the lower section of the Wohlwillstrasse with its terraced residential project in the Jägerpassage. And at the hub are Café Stark, Strips & Stories, the Suicycle bicycle shop and the Kandie Shop. Here you can relax, enjoy a cup of fair-trade coffee and home-made carrot cake. Or if the weather cooperates, sit outside on the street-side benches.

Hamburg wäre nicht Hamburg ohne die ehemals besetzten Häuser an der Hafenstraße, die bis heute als genossenschaftliches Eigentum der Glas-und-Stahl-Perlenkette an der Elbe trotzen. Als die Häuser in den 1980ern zum Abriss vorgesehen waren, lieferten sich die Bewohnerinnen und Bewohner jahrelang erbitterte Kämpfe mit der Polizei und der Stadtverwaltung, die die Häuser heute wegen ihrer „bunten Fassaden" und „bewegten Historie" als Sehenswürdigkeit vermarktet. Wer sich für die Details der Häuserkämpfe interessiert, findet im Archiv der Sozialen Bewegung in der Roten Flora umfangreiches Quellenmaterial.

Hamburg would not be Hamburg without its one-time squatted buildings in the Hafenstrasse. Today they are still collectively-owned properties situated in the row of glass and steel façades lining the Elbe. The buildings were slated for demolition in the 1980s but local residents waged a bitter battle with the police and the city government to save them. Now the city proudly touts the same buildings as city sights, known for their "colorful façades" and "moving history." Anyone interested in the history of the struggle will find loads of documentation in the Archive of the Social Protest in the Rote Flora. **asb.nadir.org**

St. Pauli ist St. Pauli ist St. Pauli — der britische *Guardian* hat den Stadtteil vor ein paar Jahren zu einem der fünf lebenswertesten Orte der Welt gekürt. Und wozu? Zu Recht. Wem das bei einem Besuch wirklich nicht spontan einleuchtet, kann sich bei einer der thematischen Touren des St. Pauli Tourist Office erklären lassen, was so toll ist an St. Pauli — von Leuden, die ihr Viertel lieben.

St. Pauli is St. Pauli is St. Pauli. A few years ago, the British Guardian newspaper declared the area to be one of the five most livable places in the world. And why? Because it's true. Any visitor who doesn't see that right away can take a theme tour from the St. Pauli tourist office and get an explanation of why the neighborhood is so great—from the people who live there and love their neighborhood. **pauli-tourist.de**

Millerntor-Stadion
Feldstraße 1, 20359 St. Pauli

Auch (oder gerade) wenn man sich gar nicht für Fußball interessiert, sollte man sich wenigstens einmal ein Spiel des „Weltpokalsiegerbesiegers" im heimatlichen Stadion ansehen. Geschicktes „Retter"-Marketing hat den FC St. Pauli vor ein paar Jahren vor der Pleite gerettet, und auch wenn Marketing und Fankultur heute kaum noch auseinanderzuhalten sind, hat der Verein sein lokalpatriotisches Cool, das ihn spätestens seit der Solidarisierung mit den Kämpfen um die Hafenstraßenhäuser wie eine Piratenfahne umweht, nicht verloren.

If you are interested in soccer, or not, you should at least go see one home game of the "World Club Champion beaters," a title FC St. Pauli earned when they once beat powerhouse Bayern Munich. Clever rescue marketing meanwhile spared the cult club from bankruptcy a few years ago. And although the media hype and fan culture are now nearly indistinguishable, the club has not lost its aura of patriotic cool that dates back to the 1980s when it supported the squatted house movement in the Hafenstrasse. The team's skull and crossbones pirate flag only add to the effect. **fcstpauli.com**

21

Smallville ist ein Plattenladen/Record Label/Booking Agentur und allgemeiner Hotspot und Hangout für Menschen mit Interesse an elektronischer Musik der Richtungen House, Detroit, Techno und Electronica. Und für Fans cooler Zeichnung, möchte man fast sagen, denn Stefan Marx ist Freund und Hausgrafiker von Smallville Records. Seine toll-merkwürdigen Strichzeichnungen gibt es dort in allen Darreichungsformen — auf Plattencovern, Postern, T-Shirts, Taschen, Schaufenstern und Zines.

Smallville is a record store, record label, booking agency, all-around hotspot and hangout for people into electronic House, Detroit, Techno and Electronica music. And you could almost also say for anyone who likes cool illustration, as Stefan Marx is a friend of the shop and the go-to graphic artist for Smallville Records. They carry his beautiful, oddball line drawings in all sorts of shapes and sizes—album covers, posters, t-shirts, bags, window decals and zines.
smallville-records.com

22

Mit dem Blick auf die Elbe und den Palmen aus Metall ist Park Fiction auch schön, wenn man gar nichts über die Geschichte des kleinen Parks weiß. Aber die Aussicht ist umso schöner mit dem Wissen, dass die Anwohnerinnen und Anwohner des Viertels jahrelang für diesen Park gekämpft haben. Sie haben die bereits geplante Bebauung verhindert und stattdessen in einem künstlerischen Prozess einen selbstverwalteten, öffentlich geplanten Park gestaltet.

View of the Elbe River under fake palm trees. Park Fiction is beautiful even if you know nothing of its origins. But the view is all the more stunning when you learn that the area's residents fought for years to create this little park. They were able to stop an approved construction project and creatively replace it with a self-managed, public park. parkfiction.org

Cap San Diego
Überseebrücke, 20459 St. Pauli

Die Cap San Diego, der „weiße Schwan des Süd-atlantiks", ist nicht nur das größte seetüchtige Museumsfrachtschiff der Welt, sondern auch ein Veranstaltungsort mit abwechslungsreichem kulturellen Programm. Ein besonderer Clou: Man kann an Bord des schnittigen Stückgutfrachters übernachten und darf sich dabei auf dem Passagierdeck mit Speisesaal, Schwimmbad und Poolbar fühlen wie ein eleganter Reisender auf Südamerika-Passage.

The Cap San Diego, the "White Swan of the Southern Atlantic," is not just the largest seaworthy museum cargo ship in the world. The vessel is also a cultural venue with an exciting program. A special highlight: on board the sleek cargo freighter, you can stay overnight, lounge on the passenger deck with dining room, swimming pool and tiki bar and pretend like you are a first-class passenger on a sailing to South America. capsandiego.de

Kleine Pause
Wohlwillstraße 37, 20359 St. Pauli

Weil die Kleine Pause direkt an der Verbindungs-strecke zwischen Schanze und Reeperbahn liegt, treffen sich hier Stammgäste aus der Nachbarschaft und wanderndes Partyvolk. Das Kerngeschäft sind spitzenmäßige „Pommes Schranke", großzügige Burger und leckere hausgemachte Salate alter Schule („Gurkensalat in weißer Tunke").

The Kleine Pause's location on a connecting street between the Schanzenviertel neighborhood and the Reeperbahn draws both local regulars from around the block and itinerant bar hoppers.

KAUFEN KAUFEN KAUFEN

Nö zur Mö — Alternativen zur Mönckebergstraße
Shop till you drop—more than just Mönckebergstrasse

Lange Reihe oben indisch-portugiesisch, unten edel-gay
Indian-Portuguese upper section, chic-gay lower section
Colonnaden Schlendern unterm Säulengang
stroll under the portico
Schulterblatt/Susannenstraße/Schanzenstraße
früher punk rock, heute the place to be
used to be punk rock, now the place to be
Eppendorfer Weg endlos lang und für alle
goes on forever, and something for everyone
Lehmweg/Eppendorfer Baum Shopping für die Ladies
ladies' shopping paradise
Mühlenkamp reife Schönheit an der Alster
middle-aged beauty on the Alster
Kohlhöfen rising star oberhalb des Gängeviertels
rising star in the vicinity of Gängeviertel
Marktstraße irgendwie ganz anders, immer noch
somehow still original, even now
Weidenallee Shoppen und Chillen für Leute ab dreißig
shopping and chilling out for the over-thirty crowd
Osterstraße kleine Läden, große Ketten *small shops, large chains*
Ottenser Hauptstraße familiär und gediegen
good for families and sophisticated
Fuhlsbüttlerstraße schön normal, mit Euroshops
nice and normal, with discount euro shops
Neuer Wall Gucci, Prada & Konsorten *Gucci, Prada & company*
Waitzstraße „Alexandra's", „Giorgio's", „Bettina Mode"

Menu standards are terrific "Pommes Schranke" (fries with ketchup and mayonnaise), copious burgers and traditional German homemade salads, such as "Cucumber salad in white sauce." **kleine-pause.de**

Schüllenbach Ferd.
Budapester Straße 49, 20359 St. Pauli

„Ferd." hat alles. Und auch wenn man mit Eisenwaren nichts am Hut hat, sollte man dort wenigstens ein Mal nach einer ganz bestimmten Schraube fragen, um mit hinten ins Lager gehen zu dürfen. Da türmen sich Tausende von Kleinteilen in endlosen Regalen – beeindruckend, dass die Mitarbeiter wissen, was wo liegt. Vorne im Laden sitzt eine geborene Schüllenbach persönlich in ihrem kleinen Kassenhäuschen und zieht die 35 Cent ab, die die Schraube dann kostet.

"Ferd." has it all. And even if you are not that interested in hardware, you should visit at least once to ask for some impossible-to-find screw. That's your ticket to a tour of the stockroom. Thousands of parts and pieces piled high in never-ending shelves. Unbelievable that the staff can find anything at all. A real member of the Schüllenbach clan sits up front in an enclosed cashier booth to tender your 35 cents for the screw.

Kunst Kiosk
Paul-Roosen-Straße 5, 22767 St. Pauli

Anders als die seriell gefertigten Design-Produkte der vielen neuen Concept Stores sind die Waren im Kunst Kiosk eher der d.i.y.- und craft-Kultur verpflichtet, und man sieht ihnen ihre handgemachten Qualitäten an. Die beiden Inhaberinnen sind selbst Gestalterinnen, im Laden stehen die eigenen Produkte, andere Künstlerinnen und Designer können sich in ihrem Kiosk einmieten. Das Ergebnis ist ein vielfältiges Angebot an schönen Dingen auf hohem gestalterischen Niveau.

Unlike the mass-manufactured design products in the many new concept stores, Kunst Kiosk is the best address for D.I.Y. and indie crafts that really look hand-crafted. Both store owners are themselves designers and offer their own crafts, but they also rent out space to other artists and designers. The result is a colorful range of beautiful things at a sophisticated artistic level.
kunstkiosk-hamburg.de

27

Freiheit & Roosen mit dephekt
Paul-Roosen-Straße 41, 22767 St. Pauli

Das Angebot von Freiheit & Roosen ist eklektisch und mysteriös: Zwar sind zwischen den Vinyltrögen und den alten Abspielgeräten nur schmale Gänge frei, aber in den übervollen Altbauräumen gibt es neben Platten und „Technik zum Liebhaben" auch alles mögliche andere: alte Bücher, aber auch verlagsneue, Lampen und Dekokitsch aus den Fünfzigern, aber auch die aktuelle Ausgabe der Szene Hamburg, analoge Kameras und anderer Leute Mixtapes.

The inventory in Freiheit & Roosen is eclectic and mysterious: the aisles weave a narrow path between bins of vinyl and old stereo equipment. But besides records and "technologies you love to love," the overcrowded rooms of this store in a historic building have just about everything else: old books, brand-new ones, lamps and decorator kitsch from the fifties, right alongside the current edition of Szene Hamburg, plus film cameras and other people's mixtapes.

28

Kleine Freiheit No. 1
Kleine Freiheit 1, 22767 St. Pauli

Vier Freundinnen haben sich zusammengetan und geben in der Kleinen Freiheit 1 ihrer breiten Erfahrung in der Mode- und Designbranche eigenen Raum. Hinten schneidern sie die lässigen Teile für ihr Streetwear-Label [iksi:], die sie vorne im Laden neben skandinavischer Mode, ausgewählter

Vintagewear und hauseigenen Accessoires verkaufen (die Einzelstücke von Jonnygold Jewelry werden hier hergestellt). Noch mehr
Abwechslung kommt ins Haus, weil die Inhaberinnen ihren Laden
regelmäßig für Popup-Stores und andere Events untervermieten.

*Four girlfriends teamed up to create this store at Kleine
Freiheit 1 as an outlet for their broad experience in the fashion and
design industries. In the back, they confect casual pieces for their
streetwear label [Iksi:]. These are sold up front, along with Scandinavian fashion, selected vintage wear and made-in-house accessories
(Jonnygold Jewelry one-of-a-kind pieces are produced here). Actually, this shop is all about variety—the owners regularly loan out the
premises for pop-up stores and other events.* **kleinefreiheit1.de**

Kombüse
Bernhard-Nocht-Straße 51, 20359 St. Pauli

Echt? Unecht? Egal! In der Kombüse sieht es fast
aus wie in einer echten Schiffskombüse – wenn
nur die „Stahlträger" nicht nach Holz klingen
würden und die „genietete" Decke nicht mit Raufaser tapeziert
wäre. Die riesigen Tex-Mex-Burritos, die dort serviert werden, sind
auch nicht unbedingt echt, jedenfalls nicht echt mexikanisch, aber
dafür echt lecker. Hinterher kann man nebenan in der Kogge noch
schön einen Tresenschnaps zur Verdauung trinken – muss man
dann auch, bei den Portionen.

*Is it real? Fake? Whatever! In the Kombüse, which
means ship's galley in German, it looks so nautically authentic—if
only the "steel beams" weren't made out of wood and the "riveted
ceiling" wasn't covered with wood-chip wallpaper. The huge Tex-Mex
burritos are not necessarily the real deal either, at least not authentic Mexican, but they are really good. Afterwards, head for the Kogge
next door for a nice after-dinner brandy at the bar, which you'll need,
given Kombüse's sizable portions.*

Otzentreff
Otzenstraße 4, 20359 St. Pauli

Hinter den Buntglasfenstern hat an Silvester früher die Nachbarschaft unter Girlanden zu Schlagern geschunkelt. Inzwischen haben junge Anhänger des FC St. Pauli den Otzentreff in eine Fankneipe verwandelt, aber am Interieur wurde nicht viel gemacht: Die wenigen Tische rund um den Tresen sind mit riffeligem Kupferblech bezogen und die Wände hellgelb verschalt, es wird geraucht wie eh und je, und manchmal laufen auch noch Schlager, ironisch natürlich.

This bar once throbbed to the strains of Schlager, the sentimental German ballads that reached their apogee in the 1960s and 70s. Then it was bought by a group of young FC St. Pauli supporters who turned it into a "fan bar," but who left the interior pretty much unchanged, complete with copper-topped tables, pale yellow paneling, and cigarette smoke. They still play Schlager every now and then, but in a postmodern, ironic kind of way.

Wohlers Park
Bei der Johanniskirche 10, 22767 Altona

Ein bisschen komisch ist es schon, zwischen den Grabplatten zu sitzen und zu grillen. Oder sich sogar draufzulegen und sich zu sonnen. Es ist leichter, die Skrupel zu überwinden, wenn man weiß, dass auf dem ehemaligen Friedhof Norderreihe schon seit 1945 niemand mehr begraben wurde. Und dass diese letzten Ruhestätten in der Nachkriegszeit zum Gemüseanbau genutzt wurden und die grünen Schattenspender als Brennholz. Seit 1978 ist der Friedhof eben ein Park – mit Alleen und Mausoleen.

It's a little weird to sit down for a barbeque surrounded by—or maybe even sunbathing on—the stone slabs of a graveyard. But it helps ease the conscience a bit to know that no one has been buried here at the site of the former Norderreihe Cemetery since 1945. And that the postwar period saw these final resting places repurposed as vegetable gardens, with shade-giving trees used for firewood. Since 1978, the cemetery is just a park—with little paths and mausoleums.

Klassische Fahrräder
Bernstorffstraße 148, 22767 Altona

Drin ist, was draufsteht: Oliver Zschirnt verkauft Klassische Fahrräder – Rennräder, Hollandräder, Klappräder und Oldtimer. Seine Liebe zum Detail lebt er an alten, gemufften Stahlrahmen aus und bietet in seinem schönen Laden in der Bernstorffstraße gut erhaltene und generalüberholte Fahrradklassiker der 1950er bis 1980er Jahre an.

Oliver Zschirnt sells classic bikes—racing bikes, Dutch bikes, folding bikes and vintage models. The craftsman devotes his assiduously detailed attention to old, lugged steel frames, offering well preserved and generally overhauled bicycle classics from the 1950s through 1980s in his lovely store in Bernstorffstrasse.
klassische-fahrraeder-hamburg.de

Frau Hedis Tanzkaffee
Bei den St. Pauli-Landungsbrücken 10, 20359 St. Pauli

Es schunkelt so schön auf der Hedi, vor allem wenn die kleine alte Barkasse gerade ein riesiges Containerschiff passiert hat, und die Wellen schwappen im Takt der Tanzmusik. Die Getränke muss man dann sehr gut festhalten, sich selbst manchmal auch, und vielleicht ist sich auf diese Weise bei einer Barkassenparty auf der Hedi schon so manches spätere Paar schneller nähergekommen, als es an Land ziemlich wäre.

Everything sways so nicely at Hedi's, especially when a big container ship sails by the little barge café and the waves splash in time to the music. Hold on to your drink—and to each other, too. Maybe that's the reason some couples had any easier time getting to know one another at a barge party on Hedi's than they did on shore.
frauhedi.de

34

Bermuda-Dreieck
Thadenstraße, Ecke Wohlwillstraße, 20359 St. Pauli

Ein paar Bier vom Kiosk und dann auf dem Bordstein sitzen, wo der Asphalt mit Kronenkorken gepflastert ist und die Sonne abends durch die Thadenstraßenschlucht scheint; für die Autos kaum die Füße einziehen und gucken, wer da so vorbeikommt auf dem Weg von der Schanze zum Kiez. Wer das Straßensitzen nicht mag, hat die Wahl zwischen immer mehr Restaurants, Bars und Kiosken.

A Bermuda Triangle this far north—grab a few beers from the kiosk and pull up a spot on the curb. The asphalt is strewn with bottle caps and the low evening sun blazes through the Thadenstrasse, like in a canyon. Cars nearly drive over a few feet as you watch the comings and goings between St. Pauli and the hip Schanzenviertel neighborhood. Don't like sitting on the ground? There are plenty of restaurants, bars and beverage kiosks to choose from.

35

Fritzis Osteria
Kleine Freiheit 1, 22767 St. Pauli

Irgendwer musste es einfach tun. Irgendwer musste sich darum kümmern, dass die ganzen Kreativen aus den Ladenbüros in der Kleinen Freiheit ein vernünftiges Mittagessen bekommen und einen gemütlichen Ort für ihre Kaffeepause. Und Isabell Kmiecik hat es dann eben gemacht. In ihrer vintage-minimalistischen Osteria sitzt man vorne am alten 50er-Jahre-Schaufenster oder hinten auf der Eckbank und bekommt von Montag bis Freitag einfach gutes Essen.

Somebody had to do it. Somebody had to see to it that all the creatives from the storefront offices that line Kleine Freiheit could get a decent lunch or enjoy a cup of coffee in a nice ambiance. And Isabell Kmiecik went ahead and did it. Take a seat up front in the 1950s shop window of her vintage-minimalist osteria or slide on to the corner bench in the back and just enjoy good food from Monday to Friday. fritzis-osteria.com

Critical Mass
Überall

Aufregender als bei einer Radtour mit mehreren Tausend Teilnehmern kann man Hamburg gar nicht entdecken. Weil die Fahrradfahrer bei einem **36** Critical-Mass-Ride eben eine kritische Masse bilden, bleibt ihnen gar nichts anderes übrig, als auf der Straße zu fahren. Manche sagen, sie stören den Verkehr, aber nein: Sie sind der Verkehr. Mitfahren können alle, auch wenn das eigene Rad noch so oll ist, der Startpunkt für die Tour wird jeweils kurz vor jedem letzten Freitag des Monats im Internet bekanntgegeben.

There is no more exciting way to discover Hamburg than on a bike ride together with several thousand riders. Since cyclists on a Critical Mass ride are just that, namely a critical mass, they have no other choice but to ride on the road. Some say they obstruct the flow of traffic. But no—they are the traffic flow. Anyone can join in, even on the crummiest bike. The starting point for the ride is announced on the Internet just before the last Friday of the month. criticalmass-hamburg.de

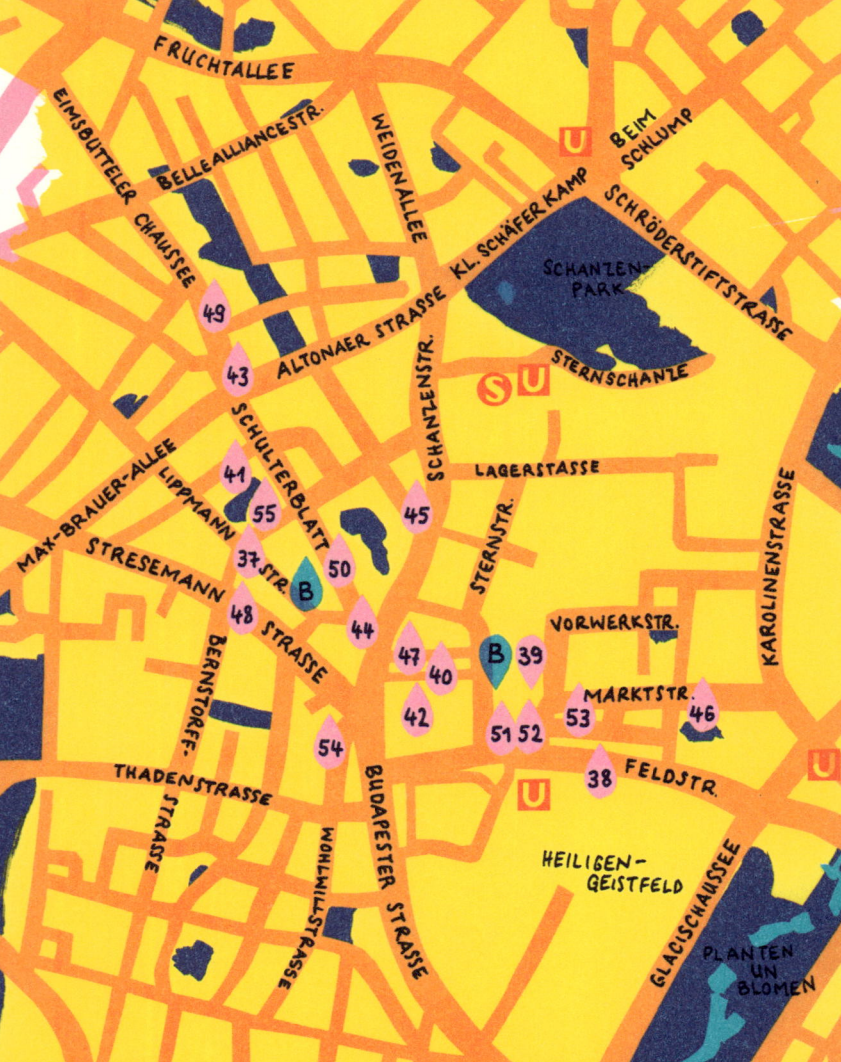

Wie es Euch gefällt
Juliusstraße 16, 22769 Hamburg St. Pauli

Wenn man unter Hamburger Freunden nach einem guten Klamottenladen fragt, sagen garantiert gleich mehrere: „Dieser Laden in der Juliusstraße, die Frau, die das macht, ist total nett." Diese Frau, die das macht, Nina Wirtz, ist aber nicht nur total nett, sondern sie ist auch Modedesignerin und hat ein professionelles Händchen dafür, in ihrer Boutique eine tolle Auswahl an Mode, Schmuck und Accessoires so zusammenzustellen, wie es uns gefällt.

If you ask your friends in Hamburg about a good clothing store, you can bet that a few will say right away: "This store in the Juliusstrasse. The woman who runs it is totally nice." This woman who runs it, Nina Wirtz, is not just totally nice. She is also herself a fashion designer and has a professional flair for stocking a great selection of fashion, jewelry and accessories—just as we like it.

wieeseuchgefaellt.blogspot.de

Karo Fisch
Feldstraße 32, 20357 Karoviertel

Zum Thema Fischimbiss gibt es eigentlich nicht viel zu sagen. Wichtig ist, dass der Fisch frisch ist und gut gebraten, dass er von klassischen Beilagen (Pommes und Salat) begleitet und flott und freundlich serviert wird. Zu viel kosten soll er auch nicht. Also alles ganz genau wie bei Karo Fisch.

A fish snack bar is not a very complicated concept. What is important is that the fish is fresh and crispy tasty, served with classic sides (fries and salad) and the service is fast and friendly. And it should not be expensive either. And that is exactly what you'll get at Karo Fisch.

39

Flexibles Flimmern
Sternstraße 4, 20357 Karoviertel

Man könnte Holger Kraus als eine Art Locationscout bezeichnen, allerdings spürt er nicht Drehorte auf, sondern Vorführorte. Mit seinem mobilen Kino zeigt er bei seiner Veranstaltungsreihe „Flexibles Flimmern" Filme in thematisch passender Umgebung. Film und Vorführung überblenden sich dabei zu einer Gesamtinszenierung, die auch oft gesehene Klassiker noch mal in einem ganz anderen Licht erscheinen lässt.

You could say that Holger Kraus is a type of location scout. But he is on the lookout for places to screen films rather than shoot them. In his mobile cinema, Flexibles Flimmern, he shows films in settings that fit the storyline, which dovetail to create an entirely original production, often casting old classics in a completely different light.
flexiblesflimmern.de

40

Schuhwunschbäume
Augustenpassage, 20357 Sternschanze

Das Liebesglück ist einem angeblich ewig hold, wenn man es mit einem gravierten Vorhängeschloss an einer Brücke sichert. Dieser merkwürdige Brauch hat sich schon herumgesprochen. Weniger bekannt ist dagegen der Glaube, man habe einen Wunsch frei, wenn man ein Paar aneinander gebundene Schuhe so in einen Baum wirft, dass sie an einem Ast hängen bleiben. An den Schuhwunschbäumen in der Augustenpassage kann man sein Glück versuchen.

Love is supposed to last forever when it is padlocked to a bridge with an engraved lock. This curious custom of lovelocks is meanwhile a wide-spread phenomenon. Less well-known is that throwing a pair of shoes up onto a tree branch, laces tied, grants you one wish. Make your wish come true at the Shoe Wish trees in the Augustenpassage.

Lokaldesign
Schulterblatt 85, 20357 Sternschanze

Es gibt viele tolle Designläden in Hamburg, aber für Lokaldesign ist toll gar kein Ausdruck. Die Inhaberin Katharina Roedelius kooperiert mit Designhochschulen und hilft Studenten, ihre guten Ideen bis zur Produktreife zu entwickeln. In jedes einzelne Möbelstück ist die ganze Energie eines anderen Jungdesigners geflossen, dementsprechend ist das Gesamtenergieniveau in dem schönen Eckladen sehr hoch. Die Super-Ideen-Dichte ist hier vielleicht die höchste von ganz Hamburg.

There are lots of great design shops in Hamburg, but great is an understatement when it comes to Lokaldesign. Owner Katharina Roedelius works with art and design schools and helps students turn their good ideas into actual products. Each piece of furniture is the culmination of another young designer's creativity, which makes for a very high energy level in this beautiful corner store. Lokaldesign probably has the highest density of great ideas in all of Hamburg. lokaldesign.de

Azeitona
Beckstraße 17-19, 20357 Sternschanze

Innen weich und würzig, außen kross und gerade eben frisch frittiert — so müssen Falafel sein. Genau deswegen, und obwohl das Falafelangebot in der Schanze kaum zu überschauen ist, solte man Falafel nicht *irgendwo* essen, sondern nur bei Azeitona. Dort gibt es jedenfalls die besten. So isses einfach.

Inside fluffy and spicy, outside crisp and fried up fresh—that's how falafel has to be. And that's exactly what you get at Azeitona. And while it is nearly impossible to keep track of all the falafel places in the Schanze neighborhood, don't get your falafel from just anywhere. Head straight for Azeitona. They have the best anyhow. That's just how it is.

43

Genbrug Gebrauchtwarenkaufhaus
Schulterblatt 116, 20357 Sternschanze

Bei Genbrug findet man manch schönes Stück. Vom 50er-Jahre-Möbel bis zum schnöden 10er-Schraubenschlüssel gibt es in diesem unaufgeregten, aber sehr gut sortierten Gebrauchtwarenkaufhaus alles, und zwar in gut erhaltenem Zustand. Aber Achtung, auch wenn es wirkt wie auf einem Designflohmarkt – handeln lohnt nicht, verkauft wird zu Festpreisen, die sind in den meisten Fällen aber völlig ok.

Genbrug's has some great finds. This well-stocked, no-hype second-hand department store has everything from 1950s furniture to the plain old 10-piece wrench set, and in good condition. Warning: even though the store might look a designer flea market, don't try to bargain. Everything is sold at fixed prices, which are usually really good deals.

44

Herr Max
Schulterblatt 12, 20357 Schanzenviertel

Der ehemalige Milchladen auf dem Schulterblatt mit seinen weiß glasierten Kacheln und blauen Bordüren sieht wirklich aus wie eine Hochzeitstorte. Während vor den großen Schaufenstern das Schanzenvolk vorbeizieht, sitzt man im Innern dieser liebevoll eingerichteten Torte und genießt klassische Konditorkunst „with a twist": Kirsch-Rosmarin-Tartes, Basilikum-Eis oder selbstgemachtes Abendbrot.

The former dairy store on Schulterblatt street looks like a wedding cake, all decked out in white glazed tiles with blue border icing. While outside the Schanze crowd strolls by the shop's big windows, there you sit inside this beautifully decorated cake and enjoy classic desserts but "with a twist"—cherry-rosemary tarts, basil ice cream or supper with Herr Max's homemade bread. **herrmax.de**

3001 Kino
Schanzenstraße 75, 20357 Sternschanze

Der schöne Saal des 3001 Kinos liegt im Hinterhof-
herzen der Schanze und bietet nicht mal hundert
Besuchern Platz. Auf dem Programm steht eine her-
vorragende Auswahl an Filmen und Filmreihen, Dokumentarfilmen
und Originalfassungen. Im Sommer organisiert das Kino die Film-
nächte im Millerntor-Stadion. Dieses ganz große Kino auf den Stadi-
ontribünen sollte man sich nicht entgehen lassen, besonders wenn
direkt nebenan mal wieder der Sommerdom tobt.

*The beautiful theater of the 3001 Kino cinema is nestled
within one of the Schanze district's many courtyard buildings, with
seating for less than one hundred movie-goers. The program features an excellent selection of film series, films and documentaries
and original foreign language films. Come summer, the cinema organizes the movie nights in Millerntor-Stadium. This huge cinema
on the stadium bleachers is not to be missed, especially when the
Sommerdom carnival is in full force next door.* **3001-kino.de**

Lockengelöt
Marktstraße 119, 20357 Karoviertel

Die Designs, für die die Jungs vom Lockengelöt
Alltagsgegenstände zweckentfremden, versteht
man nicht nur auf einen Blick, sondern auch auf
ein Wort. Denn ihre prägnanten Bezeichnungen sind Bestandteil der
Produkte — die aus alten Büchern gefertigten Schlüsselbretter etwa
heißen „Schlüsselromane". Ein Schlüssel des Erfolgs ist es, dass sie
ihre anfängliche Verpeiltheit mit hoher Professionalität unter einen Hut gebracht haben, der Beweis dafür, dass sie in ihrer eigenen
Werkstatt im Hamburger Umland inzwischen viel fürs Ausland pro-
duzieren: Wer sonst exportiert schon Ölfässer — „Schränks" — von
Deutschland nach Amerika und Russland?

Take one look and you get it right away—the designs from the guys at Lockengelöt distort the function of common objects in a whole new direction. And the pithy product names only add punch. The key hangers made from old books are called "Schlüsselromane," a pun in German for Roman à clef. A key to their success is that they have coupled their initial flakiness with a high level of professionalism, proven by the fact that they now produce a lot of merchandise for export in their own workshop outside of Hamburg. Who else exports oil barrel cupboards from Germany to America and Russia? lockengeloet.com

Under Pressure
Schanzenstraße 10, 20357 Sternschanze

Under Pressure versorgt „die Kids" mit allem, was Hip-Hopper und Sprayer brauchen — „Streetfashion, Sneaker, Recordz, Canz" und guter Beratung vom freundlichen Fachpersonal. Laien finden bei Under Pressure ein tolles Angebot an Sneakern, Streetart- und Designbüchern, ugly toys und bedruckten T-Shirts, vor allem von Cleptomanix. Und sie werden genauso nett beraten.

Under Pressure is the hip-hopper's dream one-stop shop. "Street Fashion, Sneakers, Recordz, Canz" and good advice from the friendly staff. Both initiates and novices will find a great selection of sneakers, street art and design books, ugly toys and T-shirts, especially from Cleptomanix—and friendly advice for all. underpressure.de

Superbude
Juliusstraße 1, 22769 St. Pauli

Voll super: Die beiden Hostels an der Schanze und in St. Georg sind echt entspannt. Stress wird grundsätzlich vermieden, und auch auf Sonderwünsche reagiert das Personal gelassen: Drei Zustellbetten im Zweibettzimmer? Das geht. In der Rockstar Suite der Superbude St. Pauli braucht man die aber gar nicht, denn mit sechs Metern ist das Bett dort wirklich superbreit. Oder sagen wir: angemessen.

Absolutely awesome: the two hostels in the Schanze and St. George are really laid-back. Stress is shunned and the staff is pretty mellow when it comes to special requests. Three extra beds in a twin room? Sure. But you won't need any extra beds in the Rock Star Suite in the Superbude St. Pauli. The six-meter one there is pretty much wide enough. Or should we say fitting? **superbude.de**

Human Empire Shop
Schulterblatt 132, 20357 Eimsbüttel

Bedruckte T-Shirts, skandinavische Wohnaccessoires, Design-Bücher und Hipster-Beutel – das ist alles gut und schön im Human Empire Shop. Aber dass man dort auch die charmanten, retroavantgardistischen Poster von Human Empire bekommt (die mit den unverkennbaren Männchen mit Winkelnase, freundlichem Lächeln und Augen zu), das ist wirklich das Beste.

Printed T-shirts, Scandinavian home accessories, designer stationary and hipster bags—those are all good things at the Human Empire Shop. But this is also the place to get those charming, retro-modern Hamburg posters—the one with the funny, little man, captain's hat, friendly smile and eyes closed. And that is really great. **humanempireshop.com**

Brunos Käseladen
Schulterblatt 60, 20357 Sternschanze

Es riecht ein bisschen säuerlich wie in einer Milchkammer, und auf dem Tresen liegen die Käseräder. Eine fachliche Beratung gibt es bei Bruno oft so, dass er statt vieler Worte einfach ein Stück zum Probieren über die Theke reicht, denn seine Käseauswahl ist groß, und die Geschmäcker sind bekanntlich verschieden. Wahrscheinlich ist gleich das Richtige dabei.

The air smells pungent, like in a dairy and the counter is piled high with cheese wheels. At Bruno's, the advice on what to buy often comes as a sample of cheese rather than a lengthy explanation—there are so many cheeses to choose from and everyone has their own taste. Chances are you'll find the right one in no time.

Galerie der Schlumper
Marktstraße 131, 20357 Karoviertel

Ist das Kunst? Für den Künstler Rolf Laute war das noch nie eine Frage und so gründete er 1984 mit „werkstattunfähigen" und „psychiatrieerfahrenen" Klienten der „Alsterdorfer Anstalten" die „Schlumper". Heute verdienen sich 24 Künstler mit unterschiedlichen Behinderungen in der Alten Rinderschlachthalle in St. Pauli ihren Lebensunterhalt mit Malerei. Während der Galeriezeiten kann man mit ihnen ins Gespräch kommen oder einfach dabei zusehen, wie sie mit vollem Einsatz malen.

Is it art? For artist Rolf Laute, that was never a question. In 1984, he founded "Die Schlumper" for clients of the Alsterdorf psychiatric hospitals who have "job-related disabilities" and "contact with psychiatry." Today 24 artists with varying disabilities earn their living as painters in the studio housed in this old slaughterhouse in St. Pauli. During gallery hours, you can meet them in person or simply watch as they are deeply immersed in creating their art. **schlumper.de**

Hanseplatte
Neuer Kamp 32, 20357 Karoviertel

Analog, lokal, stationär: Die Jüngeren halten das für ein originelles Konzept der Musikverbreitung, die Älteren freuen sich über dieses Asyl der Plattenkultur – geliebt wird die Hanseplatte deshalb von allen. Die Musik im Laden kommt „von hier" und wird ergänzt durch Sachen,

„die man als Hamburger mögen muss". Außerdem gibt es maritime Mode und nettes Zeug, Bücher und ab und zu kleine Ladengigs. Sehr zu empfehlen ist der Newsletter, mit dem Hans E. Platte nicht nur auf die neu eingetroffene Musik hinweist, sondern auch allgemeine Betrachtungen zum Lauf der Welt anstellt.

Analog, local, brick-and-mortar: young people think this is an original concept for music distribution. The older ones are happy about this vinyl sanctuary. Indeed, Hanseplatte is loved by one and all. The music in the store is from "here," supplemented with music "that any Hamburger has to like." Otherwise, they also have nautical apparel and cute stuff, books and sometimes small in-store gigs. The newsletter is highly recommended, in which Hans E. Platte not only plugs the new arrivals but also speculates at large on the course of the world. **hanseplatte.de**

Druckdealer
Marktstraße 102, 20357 Karoviertel

Im Keller unterm Hochparterre liegt das Herz der Ladengalerie, die Druckwerkstatt. Dort stellen die Druckdealer seit über zehn Jahren die markanten Siebdruckwerke her, die sie oben im Laden verkaufen: T-Shirts, Hoodies, Taschen, Karten, Kissen, Poster. Das Angebot an eigenen Sachen wird von Ausstellungen, selbstvertriebenen Comics und Siebdruckoriginalen vor allem von Hamburger Zeichnerinnen und Künstlern ergänzt.

The heart of this shop-gallery, a printing workshop, is in the basement under the mezzanine first floor. Here is where this printer has been creating its striking silkscreen products for over ten years, all sold in the store upstairs: T-shirts, hoodies, bags, cards, cushions, posters. The shop's own range is supplemented by exhibitions, DIY comics and silkscreen originals, mainly by Hamburg illustrators and artists. **druckdealer.de**

Slim Jims
Bei der Schilleroper 1–3, 22767 Sternschanze

Abends ist es bei Slim Jims oft sehr voll. Normal, denn die Pizza schmeckt super und die Stimmung ist familiär und gut. Die beiden Pizzen der Woche vereinigen Zutaten, deren Kombination nicht immer naheliegend, aber immer wohlschmeckend ist. Wer's individueller, weniger experimentell oder vegan mag, stellt die Beläge für den knusprig-dünnen Boden selbst zusammen.

Slim Jims is often packed on evenings. That's normal. The pizza tastes great and the atmosphere is friendly and fun. The two pizzas of the week feature unusual ingredient combos, but they are always a treat. Those who prefer less experimental or vegan pizza can choose their own toppings for the crispy crust. **slim-jims.com**

Rote Flora
Achidi-John-Platz 1, 20357 Sternschanze

Als autonomes Kulturzentrum ist die Rote Flora über die Stadtgrenzen hinaus bekannt und bei manchen auch berüchtigt. Drin waren aber auch viele Hamburger noch nie. Dabei gibt es bei Konzerten und anderen Veranstaltungen regelmäßig Gelegenheit, das seit über zwanzig Jahren besetzte ehemalige Prachttheater von innen zu sehen und sich in einer der letzten Bastionen des alten Schanzenviertels von der drumherum grassierenden Kommerzialisierung und Gentrifizierung zu erholen.

The Rote Flora's reputation—or for some, notoriety—as a left-wing cultural center reaches far beyond Hamburg. But many Hamburgers themselves have never even been there. And that despite the center's regular concerts and events that give visitors a chance to see the insides of the formerly squatted sumptuous theater building. It is one of the last bastions offering a break from the rampant commercialization and gentrification now transforming the old Schanze neighborhood. **rote-flora.de**

Elbphilharmonie
Am Kaiserkai, 20457 Hafencity

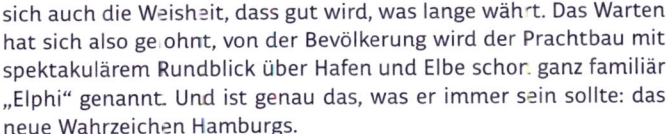

Endlich! Endlich ist sie fertig. Und wenn man einmal im großen Saal ein Konzert gehört hat, bewahrheitet sich auch die Weisheit, dass gut wird, was lange währt. Das Warten hat sich also gelohnt, von der Bevölkerung wird der Prachtbau mit spektakulärem Rundblick über Hafen und Elbe schon ganz familiär „Elphi" genannt. Und ist genau das, was er immer sein sollte: das neue Wahrzeichen Hamburgs.

At last! Finally it is finished. Anyone who has heard a concert in the Grand Hall will know that the old saying is true: good things come to those who wait. Indeed the wait was worth it, and already the stately edifice with the spectacular view of the harbor and the Elbe has been affectionately dubbed the "Elphi," making it precisely what it was always meant to be: Hamburg's new landmark.

elbphilharmonie.de

Aussichtsplattform hinter der Jugendherberge
Paula-Karpinski-Platz 3, 20354 Altstadt

Der beste Platz für typische Hamburg-Fotos? Ganz sicher der Paula-Karpinski-Platz hinter der Jugendherberge am Stintfang. Direkt oberhalb von Hamburgs Weinberg (jawohl!) hat man nämlich den besten Panoramablick über alles, was die Stadt ausmacht: die Elbe, die Schiffe, die Landungsbrücken, Hafenstraße und Speicherstadt – und neuerdings auch die Elbphilharmonie.

Where is the best place for the typical Hamburg photo, you ask? To be sure it is the view from Paula-Karpinski-Platz right behind the youth hostel on Stintfang. Just above Hamburg's vineyard (that's right!) you will find the best panoramic view of everything that makes the city special: the Elbe, the ships, the Landungsbrücken pier, Hafenstrasse and the Speicherstadt historic warehouse district and now the Elbe Philharmonic Hall as well.

58

Bei aller Liebe, Hamburg, warum würden deine besten Läden auch in Berlin oder New York nicht auffallen? Einer dieser Läden ist Gudberg Nerger. Das schicke Ladenlokal in der Poolstraße ist hinten Designagentur, „Think Tank" und Verlagssitz, an den Wänden Galerie und vorne Fachbuchhandlung mit Spezialisierung auf Künstlerbücher, Zines und besondere Printprodukte aus der Kunst- und Designecke.

Hamburg, let's face it—your best shops would also get noticed in Berlin or New York. Gudberg Nerger is one of them. The fancy store on Poolstrasse has a design agency, think tank and publisher in the back, a gallery of art hanging on the walls and a book section up front, specializing in artist books, zines and other publications from the world of art and design. **gudbergnerger.com**

59

Eigentlich ist es ja *nur* eine Stadtbücherei, aber die Zentralbibliothek am Hühnerposten verdient trotzdem eine Erwähnung. Und das nicht nur, weil sie in Hamburg unter der freundlichen Bezeichnung „Öffentliche Bücherhalle" firmiert. Im großen, ehemaligen Postbahnhof gibt es ein Café, wechselnde Ausstellungen, jede Menge Veranstaltungen, aber vor allem trifft sich Gott und die Welt mit 500 000 Medien.

Actually it's just a public library. But Hamburg's Zentralbibliothek on Hühnerposten still deserves a mention. Located in the large, former Postbahnhof train station, the library has a café, hosts exhibitions and various activities, but above all, everyone and their brother comes here to browse the some 500,000 books and media. **buecherhallen.de**

Eisenberg der Mützenmacher
Steinstraße 21, 20095 Altstadt

In dem schönen kleinen Laden ganz alter Schule sitzt Lars Küntzel und fertigt wie eh und je Hüte und Mützen von Hand. Dass der „Elbsegler" keine Gattungsbezeichnung für die bekannten blauen Schiffermützen im Schaufenster ist, sondern der Name nur eines der 18 Modelle, erklärt er mit gelassener Routine. Der Mützenmacher arbeitet vornehmlich für private Kundschaft und auf Wunsch näht er auch gern mal ein maßgeschneidertes Basecap.

In this lovely little old-school shop, owner Lars Küntzel churns out traditional handcrafted hats in eighteen different designs, like the Elbsegler, or Elbe Sailor. These are mainly for private customers, and if you ask very nicely, you might even be able to commission your own made-to-measure baseball cap.

muetzenmacher-hamburg.de

Café Johanna
Venusberg 26, 20459 Neustadt

Unter der Woche wirkt es manchmal, als sei das Café Johanna die Highend-Erweiterung der Gruner-und-Jahr-Kantine, denn das Café ist eine beliebte Alternative zum hauseigenen Angebot im Verlagsschiff um die Ecke. Man frühstückt aber auch wirklich zu schön, dort am Venusberg vor der Schaufensterfront der 50er-Jahre-Wohnblocks mit Blick ins Grüne, und kann dort nachmittags beim Cappuccino wunderbar in der Sonne sitzen.

During the week, Café Johanna is sometimes packed with employees from neighboring publishing giant Gruner + Jahr, as if it were the upscale version of their company's cafeteria. In fact, the café is a lovely place to have breakfast on the Venusberg in front of the large plate windows of this 1950s apartment building, and a great place to relax with a cappuccino when the sun is shining.

cafejohanna.de

Antik Center
Klosterwall 9–21, 20095 Altstadt

Der Mittelgang durch die ehemalige Blumenmarkthalle ist schmal, weil aus den 39 Räumen der Händler Dinge hervorquellen und lockend den Weg säumen. Man sollte viel Zeit mitbringen für das überwältigende Angebot an dunklen Möbeln, glitzernden Kronleuchtern, antiken Schmuckstücken und Büchern in Fraktur. Im Café des Antik Centers kann man sich kurz von der wohligen Reizüberflutung erholen, um sich anschließend wieder Schaulust und Sammelleidenschaft hinzugeben.

The middle aisle in this former indoor flower market is narrow because the antique dealers have stuffed their 39 showrooms to overflow and lined the walkway with enticing objects. Plan a good amount of time for the immense inventory of dark-wood furniture, glittering chandeliers, antique jewelry and books in Gothic type. The Antik Center's café is a break from the pleasant sensory overload before you resume your hunt for that must-have collector's piece.

Alternative Hafenrundfahrten
Anleger Vorsetzen, 20459 St. Pauli

Was ist eigentlich in den bunten Kisten, die da auf großen Pötten die Elbe runterfahren? Wie ist Hamburg so reich geworden? Und wer wandert durch das Tor zur Welt ein und aus? Die Hafengruppe Hamburg beantwortet solche Fragen und zeigt bei ihren politischen Hafenrundfahrten, was hinter der romantischen Hafenkulisse meist verborgen bleibt – Kolonialgeschichte, Welthandel, Migration. Vom Anleger Vorsetzen im City Sporthafen geht es auch in entlegenere Bereiche des Hafens, mitfahren kann man ohne Voranmeldung.

What exactly are in the bright boxes on those big boats chugging down the Elbe River? How did Hamburg get so rich? And who are the migrants coming and leaving through the Gateway to the World? A harbor cruise with the Hafengruppe Hamburg can answer such questions. Passengers hear about the politics and stories—colonial history, global trade, immigration—subjects that often get lost amidst all the romantic scenery. Trips depart from the Vorsetzen Pier in the City Sporthafen and also explore the harbor's more remote areas. **hafengruppe-hamburg.de**

Frau Vogel
Krayenkamp 13, 20459 Altstadt

„Souvenirs am Michel" hieß dieser Laden, bevor „Frau Vogel" ihn umkrempelte. Zwar hält sie auch weiterhin Buddelschiffe und maritime Bierseidel bereit, aber mit witzig-designigen Geschenken wie Elbphilharmonie-Ausstechformen spielt sie das Hamburg-Thema eher über Bande. Dabei gibt sie auch ihren allerpersönlichsten Vorlieben nach: Ob als lebensgroße Porzellanfigur mit Perlenkette, Fotodruck auf dem Schminkbeutel oder Fruchtgummifigur, heimlicher Herrscher im Reich der Erinnerungsstücke unterm Michel ist der Mops.

"Souvenirs am Michel" was the name of this shop before "Frau Vogel" turned it inside out. Although she still sells ships in bottles and nautical beer steins, there are also funny designer gifts such as cookie cutters in the shape of the Elbe Philharmonic Hall—the Hamburg souvenir theme but with a twist. She also indulges in her own very personal preferences: a life-size porcelain figure with pearl necklace, make-up bags with photo prints, fruit gummie candy figures. But the secret ruler in this world of memorabilia at the foot of Saint Michael's church is actually the pug dog. **frauvogel.com**

65

25hours Hotel Hafencity
Überseeallee 5, 20457 Hafencity
In diesem maritimen Designhotel machen vor allem Kurz- und Handelsreisende fest. Der Chef bekommt die Kapitänskoje mit Hafenblick, die Mannschaft schläft in etwas kleineren Kojen mit modernen Stockbetten. Im Restaurant servieren flinke Kellner in Chucks Hamburger Labskaus oder Fish & Chips, und wenn Wind und Regen durch die Straßenschluchten der Hafencity peitschen, kann man sich an der Rezeption einen Friesennerz ausleihen.

This funky, maritime-themed designer hotel caters primarily for short-stay visitors and business travelers. The "captain's cabin" offers a view of the harbor, and there are smaller rooms with luxury bunks. In the restaurant, hardworking wait staff in chucks serve things like Hamburg labskaus and fish and chips, and on rainy, windswept days you can borrow an oilskin from reception.
25hours-hotels.com/hafencity

66

Perle Store
Großneumarkt 22, 20459 Neustadt
Wenn man mal drüber nachdenkt, macht es absolut Sinn, dass dieser Concept Store „Perle" heißt. Echte Perlen sind selten, schlicht und nicht ganz billig – ganz so wie die ausgewählten Stücke internationaler Mode-, Schmuck- und Designkollektionen, die Sabine Brandt in ihren großzügigen Räumen am Großneumarkt zusammenstellt. Und auch die stilsichere Präsentation der raren Stücke gibt der Namensgebung des Ladens recht.

If you think about it, it makes perfect sense that this concept store is named "pearl." Natural pearls are rare, unpretentious and not very cheap—just like the exclusive pieces in the international fashion, jewelry and design collections that Sabine Brandt curates in her spacious rooms on Grossneumarkt. So too the stylish presentation of rare finds justifies the store's name. **perlestore.com**

Papier & Feder
Colonnaden 108, 20354 Altstadt

Zur „erlesenen Schreibkultur" gehört bei Papier & Feder alles, was man früher so zum Schreiben brauchte: Füllfederhalter von Caran d'Ache und Tinte im Fass, edles Briefpapier, Karten und Umschläge, aber auch Schreibtischaccessoires wie farblich abgestimmte Stiftebecher, Brieföffner und Löschwiegen aus Leder. Wenn man jetzt nur noch wüsste, wie man mit der Hand schreibt! PS: Besonders toll sind die Armbänder aus Tasten alter Schreibmaschinen.

Papier & Feder has everything needed to cultivate "a sophisticated writing culture"—fountain pens from Caran d'Ache, inkwells, fine stationary, cards and envelopes, as well as color-coordinated desk accessories like pencil holders, letter openers and leather ink blotters. If you only still knew how to write by hand! PS: The bracelets made out of old typewriter keys are really great.

Feinkunst Krüger
Kohlhöfen 8, 20355 Altstadt

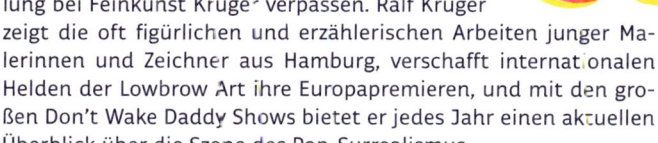

Unter keinen Umständen darf man eine Ausstellung bei Feinkunst Krüger verpassen. Ralf Krüger zeigt die oft figürlichen und erzählerischen Arbeiten junger Malerinnen und Zeichner aus Hamburg, verschafft internationalen Helden der Lowbrow Art ihre Europapremieren, und mit den großen Don't Wake Daddy Shows bietet er jedes Jahr einen aktuellen Überblick über die Szene des Pop-Surrealismus.

Not to be missed—the art exhibitions at Feinkunst Krüger gallery. Ralf Krüger shows mostly figurative and narrative

ALLES AUSSER AMAZON

Jeder Buchladen ist ein toller Ort — hier eine Liste *aller* Buchhandlungen in Hamburg (naja, *sehr* vieler). Support your local Buchladen!
Everything except Amazon: Every bookstore is a great place—here is a list of (almost all) bookshops in Hamburg. Support your local bookstore!

Auf Pauli und am Hafen
Strips & Stories
Wohlwillstraße 28
strips-stories.de

Karos und Sterne
Cohen & Dobernigg
Sternstraße 4
codobuch.de
Buchhandlung
im Schanzenviertel
Schulterblatt 55
schanzenbuch.com

Hafenspeichercity
Boysen + Mauke
Große Johannisstraße 19
schweitzer-online.de
Bucerius Kunst Forum
Rathausmarkt 2
buceriuskunstforum.de
Dr. Götze Land & Karte
Alstertor 14-18
landundkarte.de
Buchhandlung im
Haus der Photographie
Deichtorstraße 2
deichtorhallen.de

Buchhandlung Felix Jud
Neuer Wall 13
felix-jud.de
Buchhandlung
Walther König/MKG
Steintorplatz 1
buchhandlung-
walther-koenig.de
Buchhandlung am Rathaus
Rathausmarkt 7
marissal.de
Sautter + Lackmann
Admiralitätstraße 71
sautter-lackmann.de
stories! im Hanseviertel
Große Bleichen 36
stories-hamburg.de
Thalia Europa-Passage
Ballindamm 40
thalia.de
Thalia Spitalerstraße
Spitalerstraße 8
thalia.de

Anner Alster
Buchkontor Hamburg
Bogenstraße 3
buchkontor.hamburg

Bücher & Co.
Winterhuder Marktpl. 6-7
buecherco.de
Bücherstube Stolterfoht
Rothenbaumchaussee 100
Buchhandlung Heymann
Hudtwalckerstraße 35
heymann-buecher.de
KiBuLa
Schenkendorfstraße 20
kibula-hamburg.de
Buchhandlung
im Literaturhaus
Schwanenwik 38
buchhandlung-
samtleben.de
Buchhandlung
am Mühlenkamp
Mühlenkamp 39
Thalia Hamburger Straße
Hamburger Straße 25
thalia.de
Winterhuder Bücherstube
Maria-Louisen-Straße 65
winterhuder-
buecherstube.de
Buchhandlung Wohlers
Lange Reihe 68

Hamburger Osten

Buchhandlung Alte Holstenstraße
Alte Holstenstraße 24
buchalteho.de

Buchhandlung Heymann
Weidenbaumsweg 21
heymann-buecher.de

Sachsentor-Buchhandlung
Sachsentor 11
sachsentorbuch.de

Buchhandlung Seitenweise
Hammer Steindamm 113
seitenweise-hh-hamm.de

Thalia Wandsbek
Quarree 8, thalia.de

NordNordWest

Bücherstube Fuhlsbüttel
Hummelsbüttler
Landstraße 8
fuhlsbuecher.de

Das Buch in Eppendorf
Eppendorfer Landstraße 56
dasbuchineppendorf.de

Buchhandlung Heimhalt
Erdkampsweg 18
buchhandlung-
   lutz-heimhalt.de

Buchhandlung Heymann
Eppendorfer Baum 27
heymann-buecher.de

Buchhandlung Hoffmann
Fuhlsbüttler Straße 106
buch-hoffmann.de

Buchhandlung Klauder
Duvenstedter Damm 41
buchhandlung-klauder.de

Buchhandlung Hartmann
Fuhlsbüttler Straße 386
buchhandlung-hartmann.de

Hoheeimsbüttelluft

Buchhaus ABC
Hoheluftchaussee 60,
abc-buchhaus.de

Frank & Pape
Hoheluftchaussee 51
frankundsteinwarder.de

**Heinrich-Heine-
Buchhandlung**
Grindelallee 26-28
heinebuch.de

Buchhandlung Heymann
Osterstraße 134
heymann-buecher.de

Lesesaal
Lappenbergsallee 36
lesesaal-hamburg.de

Buchhandlung Lüders
Heußweg 33
buchhandlunglueders.de

**Buchladen in der
Osterstraße**
Osterstraße 171
buchladen-osterstraße.de

Päki
Hartungstraße 22
paeki.de

stories!
Straßenbahnring 17
stories-hamburg.de

Allzunah

Buchhandlung Christiansen
Bahrenfelder Straße 79
buchhandlung-
   christiansen.de

Hugendubel
Ottenser Hauptstraße 10

Schlüter'sche
Behrstraße 6

Weltbild
Bahrenfelder Straße 119

Zweieinsdrei
Große Bergstraße 213
buch-zweieinsdrei.de

Anner Elbe

Buchhandlung Harder
Waitzstraße 24

Buchhandlung Heymann
Erik-Blumenfeld-Pl. 27
heymann-buecher.de

Buchhandlung Kortes
Elbchaussee 577
kortes-buecher.de

**Buchhandlung am
Nienstedtener Markt**
Nienstedtener
   Marktplatz 28

Quotes
Waitzstraße 19
quotes-club.de

Thalia Elbe EKZ
Osdorfer Landstraße 131
thalia.de

Über die Elbe

Buchhandlung Leichers
Meyerstraße 1

Buchhandlung Lüdemann
Fährstraße 26
   luedebuch.de

Buchhandlung am Sand
Hölertwiete 5
amsand.de

Thalia Harburg
Hannoversche Straße 86
thalia.de

works of young painters and artists from Hamburg. He orchestrates European premiers for the international heroes of Lowbrow Art. And every year, he offers a current overview of the pop-surrealism scene with the great Don't Wake Daddy shows. **feinkunst-krueger.de**

69

Gängeviertel
Valentinskamp 39, 20355 Neustadt

Schon cool: Im Sommer 2009 haben rund 200 Künstlerinnen und Aktivisten ein ganzes Viertel vor dem Abriss gerettet. Dann haben sie die Stadt dazu gebracht, die bereits an einen Investor verkauften Gebäude zurückzukaufen, verhandeln seitdem über die zukünftige Nutzung. Ein so großes Projekt kann nicht ohne Widersprüche sein. So ist das Gängeviertel zwar einerseits Teil der kritischen „Recht-auf-Stadt"-Bewegung, andererseits dient es als Aushängeschild für das Marketing-Leitbild der „Kreativen Stadt". So oder so – dem Aufruf „Komm in die Gänge" für eine der vielen Veranstaltungen zu folgen lohnt sich allemal.

A pretty cool story: in summer 2009, some 200 artists and activists saved an entire neighborhood from demolition. Then they got the city to buy back the buildings it had previously sold to an investor. Since then they've been negotiating the property's future use. Such a large project is not without contradictions. The Gängeviertel area is both part of the "Right to the City" anti-gentrification movement and a hallmark for Hamburg's "Creative City" marketing campaign. Either way, it is well worth the effort to answer the call "Komm in die Gänge" (a pun on the German expression 'get a move on') and attend one of its many events. **das-gaengeviertel.info**

70

Fleetschlösschen
Brooktorkai 17, 20457 Hafencity

Das Fleetschlösschen ist zwar nie ein Schloss gewesen, aber so schön wie ein Schloss ist das ehemalige

Zollhäuschen doch. Es steht mit den Hinterbeinen im Wasser des Holländischen Brooks, hat die alten Speicher im Rücken und den zugigen Überseeboulevard vor der Nase. Hier kann man abends in der Sonne mit Werbern, Journalisten und Geschäftsleuten ein Feierabendbier trinken und die Touristengruppen beobachten, die die Hafencity bestaunen.

The Fleetschlösschen was never really a castle. But this former custom house is still just as beautiful. Its back legs stand in the current of the Holländischer Brook, the bustling Überseeboulevard at its doorstep and the old warehouses as a backdrop. Here's where you can mingle with ad industry professionals, journalists and business people for a drink after work. Or watch the tourists as they ooh and aah over Hafencity. **fleetschloesschen.de**

Grillstation Michelwiese
Schaarsteinweg 22, 20459 Neustadt
Beneidet von den Angestellten bei Gruner + Jahr nebenan, kann man auf der Michelwiese einfach drauflosgrillen. Zwar „nur" auf dem Elektrogrill und ohne echte Kohlen, aber dafür auch ohne Vorbereitung, ohne Einweggrill und ohne drohende Rauchvergiftung. Für zwei Euro bekommt man an einem der drei Grills zwanzig Minuten lang 220° und Geselligkeit mit benachbarten Grillmeistern gleich dazu. Proviant gibt es im Supermarkt im Brauerknechtgraben um die Ecke.

Employees of the giant publisher Gruner + Jahr next door look enviously on as the barbecues fire up in the Michelwiese park. Okay—"only" electric grills are allowed and with no real charcoal, but then you don't need to prepare anything, no disposable grill or danger of smoke inhalation. Two euros get you twenty minutes on one of three grills, plus the company of your neighboring barbecue chefs. Buy your supplies at the supermarket in Brauerknechtgraben street around the corner. **grill-drauf-los.de**

71

72

HVV-Haltestelle HCU
Versmannstraße, 20457 Hafencity

Die Haltestelle HafenCity Universität der neuen HVV-Linie U4 ist sozusagen das Gegenstück zur uralten U-Bahn-Station am Klosterstern. Aber weil Leben, Arbeiten und Einkaufen in der Hafencity eben noch längst nicht so selbstverständlich sind, wie die Planer sich das gedacht haben, halten sich in der hypermodernen Station oft mehr Touristen als Fahrgäste auf. Vom Zwischengeschoss aus machen sie spektakuläre Fotos von den riesigen Leuchtcontainern, die die mit Stahl verkleideten Wände und Decken in wechselnde Lichtfarben tauchen.

The new HVV U4 underground train stop at HafenCity University is essentially the opposite of the very old station at Klosterstern. But because life, work and shopping in Hafencity are not as easy as the planners of this new district imagined, more tourists than commuters make a stop at the ultra-modern station. From the mezzanine, they snap spectacular photos of the giant light box fixtures illuminating the steel-clad walls and ceilings in a non-stop color light show.

73

Milch Feinkost
Ditmar-Koel-Straße 22, 20459 Neustadt

Auch denen, die den Begriff „Third Wave Coffee" noch nie gehört haben, wird auffallen, dass der Kaffee im Milch besonders gut schmeckt. Doch Inhaber Nico Ueckermann kann nicht nur Kaffee, sondern auch Kommunikationsdesign: Das minimalistische Corporate Design und die Inneneinrichtung des Milch hat er selbst gestaltet, basierend auf dem noch vorhandenen Ladenschild des Vorgängergeschäfts, das auch Namensgeber ist. Da kann man nur sagen: Der Mann hat Geschmack.

Even those who have never heard of third-wave coffee will notice that the coffee at Milch tastes really good. Owner Nico

Ueckermann is not just a coffee expert, however; he also has a knack for communication design. He took the still-existant storefront sign from the previous business as inspiration in creating Milch's minimalist corporate design and interior as well as giving it its name. It must be said: the man has taste. **milchfeinkost.de**

Hamburger Unterwelten
Burchardstraße 22, 20095 Altstadt

Alle Welt weiß, dass es in Hamburg mehr Bunker gibt als in Venedig. Viele der Betonkolosse aus dem Zweiten Weltkrieg sind inzwischen mehr oder weniger erfolgreich ins Straßenbild integriert, aber die meisten der rund 700 Bunker liegen unter der Erde und lassen sich nur im Rahmen von Führungen erkunden. Der Verein Hamburger Unterwelten führt zum Beispiel durch den riesigen Tiefbunker am Hauptbahnhof – historische Erklärungen, technische Demonstrationen und leichte Beklemmungen inklusive.

Everyone knows that there are more bunkers in Hamburg than in Venice. Many of the mammoth concrete giants from the Second World War meanwhile blend in with the city's streetscape. But most of the some 700 bunkers below ground can only be explored through a guided tour. The Hamburg Unterwelten association will take you on tour of below-ground sites such as the huge underground bunker at the main train station—history, technical demonstrations and a slight case of claustrophobia all included. **hamburgerunterwelten.de**

Speicherstadtmuseum
Am Sandtorkai 36, 20457 Hafencity

Dieses Museum ist das Gedächtnis der Speicherstadt: Wo einst Quartiersleute und Ewerführer Kaffee, Kautschuk und Tabak die Fleete entlang- und die Speicherböden hinaufbewegten, zeigt heute das privat geführte Museum, wie die Waren gestapelt, gewogen und bemustert wurden. Außerdem veranstalten die Museumsleute zwischen Säcken und Fässern jeden Monat Lesungen historischer Krimis.

This museum is the memory of the Speicherstadt district. Where once quartermasters and dock workers transported coffee, rubber and tobacco up the canals to the warehouse floor, today the building is a privately managed museum that documents how harbor goods were stacked, weighed and sampled. What's more, the museum staff organizes monthly readings of historical crime thrillers surrounded by sacks and barrels. **speicherstadtmuseum.de**

Central Congress
Steinstraße 5–7, 20095 Altstadt

Leuten, die aus Bonn oder Aachen kommen, sowie allen übrigen Westdeutschland-Nostalgikern und Freunden des gepflegten Trinkens sei ein Besuch im Central Congress empfohlen. Wandvertäfelung aus Holz, abgehängte Decken aus Alugitter und O-förmiger Konferenztisch — das minimalistische Ambiente dieser ganz besonderen Bar atmet den Geist der alten Bundesrepublik.

Those who hail from Bonn or Aachen or anyone else with nostalgic feelings about West Germany as well as fans of sophisticated drinking culture should plan a visit to Central Congress. Wood-paneled walls, suspended aluminum-grid ceilings and a rectangular conference table all combine to create the minimalist atmosphere of this very special bar palpably imbued with the spirit of the old Federal Republic. **centralcongress.de**

Speicherstadt Kaffeerösterei
Kehrwieder 5, 20457 Hafencity

Mitten im Gastraum der Speicherstadt Kaffeerösterei saugt der Rösttrichter die Kaffeebohnen an, dann rotiert die Trommel. Das sorgt für einen konstanten

Geräuschpegel und einen unwiderstehlichen Duft. Früher wurde Kaffee im Kaispeicher D nur gelagert, aber heute veredelt der Röstmeister zehnmal täglich Rohkaffee direkt unter der Nase der Gäste, die nur darauf warten, dass die emsigen Baristi die duftenden Bohnen mit perfektem Brühdruck in ihre Tassen jagen.

There, right in the middle of the reception area of the Speicherstadt Coffee Roaster, the roasting funnel sucks in the coffee beans and the drum begins to turn. This makes for a lot of noise and an irresistible aroma. The business used to only store its coffee in quay warehouse D. But now the master coffee roaster roasts coffee ten times a day, right in front of the customers as they wait for the busy baristas to pull the perfect shot with the right amount of pressure for a great cup of coffee. **speicherstadt-kaffee.de**

Oberhafenkantine
Stockmeyerstraße 39, 20457 Hafencity

Als noch niemand an Coffee to go dachte, schenkten Kaffeeklappen Kaffee aus. Eines der letzten dieser einfachen Arbeiterlokale steht gebeugt im Oberhafen. Lkw quetschen sich daran vorbei, direkt über der Dachkante fährt die Bahn, und der kleine Backsteinbau wurde schon so oft überflutet und unterspült, dass er sich um rund neun Prozent nach vorne neigt. Das Wasser im Oberhafen riecht brackig, und es stinkt ein bisschen nach Abgasen und Dingen ohne Namen, aber die regionale Küche ist super und das Hafenflair unübertroffen.

Before anyone thought of coffee to go, the so-called Kaffeeklappen were serving coffee to the masses. One of these last remaining working-class coffee houses still stands in the upper harbor. The trucks squeeze by the street out front; trains clatter overhead. The small brick building has been flooded and washed out so often that it leans forward at a 9 percent tilt. The water in the upper harbor smells brackish. The air stinks a little bit like exhaust fumes and who knows what, but the local dishes are great and the harbor atmosphere is unbeatable. **oberhafenkantine-hamburg.de**

79

Schmuckgalerie Anne Zimmer
Winkel van Sinkel
Wexstraße 28, 20355 Neustadt

Die Zusammenstellung der Waren in diesen schönen Räumen ist etwas überraschend, bis man versteht, dass sie eigentlich zwei Läden beherbergen. Hinten gestaltet die Goldschmiedin Anne Zimmer ihre Kreationen, die sie vorne zusammen mit dem Schmuck anderer Designer ausstellt. Die andere Seite des Raumes sieht aus wie materialisiertes Internet: Bei Winkel van Sinkel ist alles ganz minimalistisch in Schwarz, Weiß und Grün, mit goldenen und kupferfarbenen Akzenten. Dort bietet Zelda Czok Amsterdamer Lifestyle an, in Form von hochwertigen Designprodukten – und Zimmerpflanzen.

The selection of items in these beautiful rooms is somewhat surprising, until you realize that they actually house two stores. In the back, goldsmith Anne Zimmer crafts her creations, which are on display in the front along with jewelry by other designers. The other part of the space looks like the Internet manifested in reality: At Winkel van Sinkel, everything is totally minimalist in black, white and green with gilded and copper-toned accents. Zelda Czok brings shoppers the Amsterdam lifestyle with high-quality designer products— and houseplants. **annezimmer.de winkelvansinkel.de**

Nord Coast Coffee Roastery
Deichstraße 9, 20459 Altstadt

Dass der olle Filterkaffee noch mal so zu Ehren kommt, war ja eigentlich klar. Und tatsächlich: Heute verkösten manche Leute ihn wie Wein und beschreiben sein vielschichtiges Aroma mit einem ähnlichen Vokabular: nussig, fruchtig, kraftvoll, mit leicht erdiger Note oder leicht süßem Nachklang. Mit diesen Aromen kennen Paula Mendes und Jörn Gorzolla sich aus, denn die beiden Inhaber von Nord Coast

rösten selbst und wissen, wie man die Nuancen der Bohnen ver-
schiedener Anbaugebiete zur Entfaltung bringt.

*It was a no-brainer to predict that good old filter coffee
would once again take a place in the spotlight. And in fact, today some
people hold coffee tastings like wine tastings, describing the brew's
complex flavor with a similar vocabulary: nutty, fruity, strong, with
a faint earthy note or slightly sweet aftertaste. Paula Mendes and
Jörn Gorzolla know how to nose their way around the stuff, because
the two owners of Nord Coast roast it themselves and are experts
in extracting the nuances of beans from different growing regions.*
nordcoast-coffee.de

Haus der Photographie
Deichtorstraße 1–2, 20095 Altstadt

Man kann sich schon nicht mehr richtig vorstellen,
dass es dieses größte Ausstellungshaus für zeitgenös-
sische Fotografie in Europa einmal nicht gegeben hat,

dabei wurde das Haus der Photographie erst im Jahr 2005 eröffnet.
Hier findet auch ein alljährliches Highlight für die vielen Hamburger
Medienschaffenden statt, die Ausstellung der „Visual Leader" aus
deutschen Magazinen, Zeitungen und Internet. Dabei wird neben
der Fachjury auch das Publikum um ein Urteil gebeten — neuerdings ohne die Kenntnis des jeweils anderen, was die Sache wesentlich spannender macht.

*It is hard to imagine that the Haus der Photographie,
the largest exhibition space for contemporary photography in Europe, was opened as late as 2005. The center also hosts an annual
highlight for many media professionals in Hamburg, the "Visual
Leader" exhibition showcasing the best work from German maga-
zines, newspapers and the Internet. Both a professional jury and the
general public are asked to cast their vote. And now independently of
each other, which makes the whole thing that much more exciting.*
deichtorhallen.de

Hanseatische Materialverwaltung
Stockmeyerstraße 41–43, 20457 Hafencity

Filmset, Messe, Ausstellung, Popkonzert — was da alles übrig bleibt! Früher ging das ausrangierte Material einfach in den Müll, aber jetzt lagert die Hanseatische Materialverwaltung es ein und gibt es günstig an neue Produktionen weiter. Die Lagerhalle tief im Oberhafen ist eine Mischung aus Fundus, Gebrauchtwarenladen und Baumarkt. Ein Besuch dort lohnt sich auch, wenn man gar nichts Bestimmtes sucht, denn die Fülle an Dingen und Requisiten bringt garantiert auf neue Ideen.

Film sets, trade shows, exhibitions, pop concerts—so many leftovers! In the old days, any unneeded stuff just ended up in the trash. But now the Hanseatische Materialverwaltung stores whatever is left behind and resells it at good prices to new events. Tucked away in the middle of the upper harbor area, the warehouse is a mixture of lost-and-found, thrift store and hardware shop. It's worth the trip even if you are not looking for anything in particular. The abundance of objects and props are guaranteed inspiration.
hanseatische-materialverwaltung.de

ViewPoint Hafencity
Grandeswerderstraße, 20457 Hafencity

Schnell! Schnell noch mal hinfahren und aus dreizehn Metern Höhe alles überblicken. Noch sieht man vom ViewPoint: die Großmarkthallen, den Hauptbahnhof, den Fernsehturm, den Michel, die Elbphilharmonie, Wilhelmsburg, die Elbbrücken und die Köhlbrandbrücke, aber bald wird diese Aussicht zugebaut sein. Apropos bauen: der ViewPoint wird immer mal wieder abgebaut und an anderer Stelle wieder aufgebaut — je nachdem, wo gerade Platz ist in der Hafencity. Also vorher prüfen, wo er gerade steht.

Quick! Go once more and see it all from a height of thirteen meters. Still to be seen from ViewPoint: the wholesale market halls, the main train station, the TV Tower, St. Michael's Church, the Elbe Philharmonic Hall, Wilhelmsburg, the Elbe bridges and the Köhlbrand bridge. But soon this view will be obstructed by new buildings. Speaking of construction, ViewPoint is periodically dismantled and set up at another location, depending on wherever there is room in Hafencity. So check its location before you go.

Miniatur Wunderland
Kehrwieder 2, Block D, 20457 Hafencity

Das Miniatur Wunderland ist nun wirklich alles andere als ein Geheimtipp. Aber es ist dennoch einen Hinweis wert, dass man dort bereits am Eingang Busladungen älterer Herren begegnet, die das Klischee vom Hobbyeisenbahner idealtypisch erfüllen und dass man an vielen Stellen hinter die Kulissen blicken kann. Da sieht man mal, wie viel Computer und Kabelage dazugehören, damit die Züge ununterbrochen fahren und die kleinen Bahnhofslichter angehen, wenn die großen Deckenlichter sich alle Viertelstunde dimmen und es Nacht wird im MiWuLa.

The Miniatur Wunderland is a far cry from an insider's tip. But it should be mentioned that just inside the entrance, you'll meet busloads of elderly gentlemen that completely fit the classic stereotype of the toy railroad hobbyist. Plus, there are many spots in Wunderland where you'll get a peek behind the scenes. That gives you an idea of just how much computer and wiring is needed to keep the trains running and the small station lights burning every 15 minutes when the overhead lights dim and nighttime descends on "MiWuLa." miniatur-wunderland.de

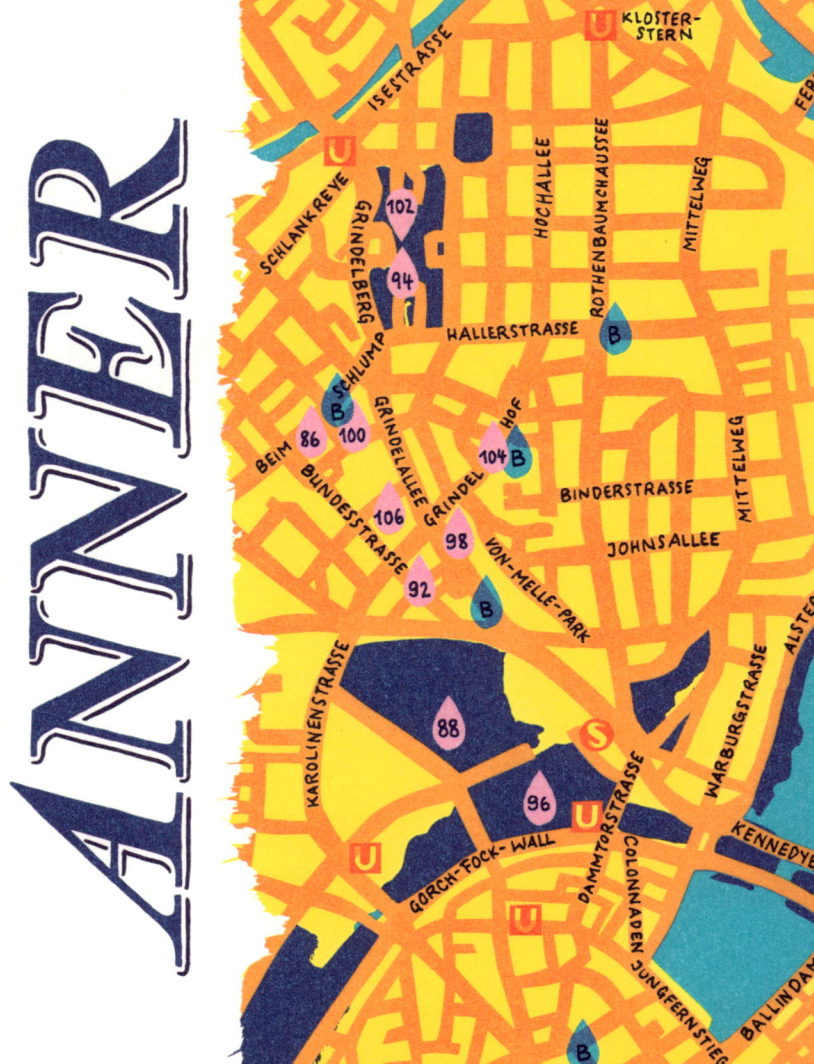

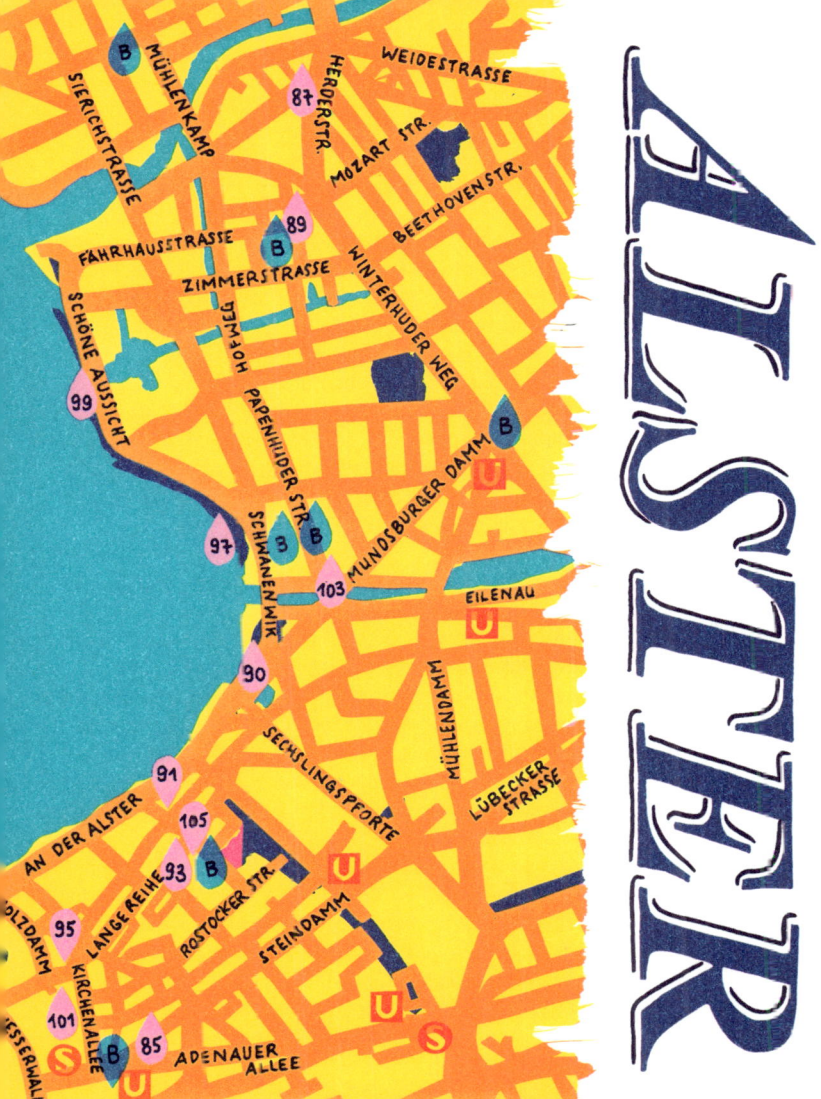

Badshah Imbiss Sweet Center
Bremer Reihe 24, 20099 St. Georg

Insider schwören, dass es im Badshah Imbiss das beste indische Essen Hamburgs gibt. Dort bekommt man auch Bombay Pakora Sandwiches, ein echtes Straßenessen und kulinarisches Hybrid aus Indiens kolonialer Vergangenheit, das in Deutschland selten angeboten wird: Was soll man auch anderes machen mit den weichen, randlosen Sandwiches der Briten, als sie mit Chutney aufzupeppen, in Pakorateig zu tauchen und im Frittierverfahren in vernünftiges Essen zu verwandeln?

Insiders claim that the Indian food at Badshah Imbiss is the best in Hamburg, and this is certainly street food at its finest. One of its specialties is the Bombay pakora sandwich, a hybrid of British and Indian colonial cuisine that you won't often see in Germany. This is a soft, crustless sandwich, with chutney for added zing, fried in pakora batter to make a deliciously calorific treat.

Karen's Konditorei
Beim Schlump 14, 20144 Eimsbüttel

Am Wochenende muss man früh aufstehen, wenn man Karens knusprige Brötchen will, ohne eine halbe Stunde lang anzustehen. Sollte die Schlange mal zu lang sein, kommt man auch in einem der Cafés in der Nachbarschaft in den Genuss der Konditoreikunst alter Schule, sie werden von Karen mit Croissants, Torten und Kuchen beliefert. Die bunten Zuckerfiguren und die Herzen aus Himbeerbaiser gibt es allerdings nur in der Konditorei selbst.

On the weekend, you have to get up early if you want Karen's crusty "brötchen" rolls without having to stand in line for half an hour. If the wait is too long, head for one of the nearby cafés to sample the old-school style bake goods of Karen, who supplies the area with croissants, cakes and pies. But only her shop sells the colorful figures in sugar and the raspberry meringue hearts.

Kaufhaus Kleinschmidt Altes + Schönes
Herderstraße 79, 22085 Uhlenhorst

Stefan Kleinschmidt hat sich auf Antiquitäten und Gebrauchtwaren der 1950er Jahre spezialisiert und präsentiert sein Angebot in einer stilechten Ladeneinrichtung in Nierentisch-Ästhetik. Weil sich der gelernte Drucker und Grafiker am liebsten originalverpackte Ware in seine Vitrinen legt, ist sein Laden nicht nur Rockabillys Traum, sondern mit all den schönen Verpackungen auch ein typografisches Wunderland.

Stefan Kleinschmidt specializes in antiques and second-hand goods from the 1950s and displays his wares in a true-to-style store, complete with the three-legged coffee table aesthetic. Because the trained printer and graphic artist prefers merchandise in its original packaging, his shop is not just a Rockabilly dream but also a typography wonderland, chocked full of packaging from the 50s.

Wasserlichtkonzerte in Planten un Blomen
St. Petersburger Straße 28, 20355 St. Pauli

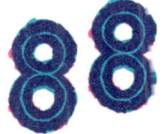

Jeden Abend von April bis Oktober spielen bei Anbruch der Dämmerung zwei Künstler die Wasserlichtorgel im Parksee von Planten un Blomen live im Takt von Musik. Die eine regelt die sprühenden Wasserstrahlen, der andere sitzt am „Lichtklavier" und beleuchtet sie bunt. Wenn klassische Musik vom Band krächzt und die bunte Fontäne 38 Meter hoch spritzt — gerade die richtige Mischung von Kitsch und Cool.

From April to October, come sunset in the Planten un Blomen park, the light organ concert begins. Two artists perform: one orchestrates the jets of water, the other plays the "light organ" to illuminate them in an array of colors. Recorded classical music plays in accompaniment to the 38-meter-high colorful fountain streams—the perfect mix of kitsch and cool.

plantenunblomen.hamburg.de/wasserlichtspiele

Delzepich Eis
Winterhuder Weg 67, 22085 Uhlenhorst

In Eintrag Nummer 166 wird zwar behauptet, dass die Eisliebe in Ottensen das beste Eis Hamburgs verkauft, aber ein Besuch bei Delzepich stellt diese Behauptung auf eine harte Probe. In dem schönen, kleinen Laden östlich der Alster gibt es eine täglich wechselnde Auswahl von hundert Sorten „pures Glück": Stachelbeer-Sorbet, Himbeer-Baiser oder Franzbröt-chen-Eis — auf ist, bis ausverkauft ist, und am nächsten Tag wird wieder frisches Eis gekocht.

Eisliebe, in Ottensen, has the best ice cream in Hamburg (see entry 166), but Delzepich Eis gives it a run for its money. This attractive little shop on the east side of the Alster offers a daily changing selection of one hundred varieties of pure happiness: gooseberry sorbet, raspberry kiss, and Franzbrötchen-Eis, which tastes like the popular butter and cinnamon pastry. Each batch is made fresh daily, so when it's gone, it's gone. delzepicheis.de

Alsterwiese am Schwanenwik
Schwanenwik, 22087 Uhlenhorst

Die Alster ist zwar längst nicht so cool wie die Elbe, aber die Aussicht von der Alsterwiese am Schwanenwik bietet eine entspannte Alternative. Gegenüber geht die Sonne unter, das Alsterwasser riecht so schön brackig nach See (ganz anders als die Elbe) und es gibt am Schwanenwik nicht nur Schwäne zu füttern, sondern auch Blässhühner, Haubentaucher, Graugänse und Möwen — mindestens.

While the Alster may not be quite as hip as the Elbe, the little lakeside park of Alsterwiese am Schwanenwik is a great place to relax, enjoy the view, and fill your nostrils with the pleasantly brackish scent of the Alster, which is quite unlike that of the Elbe. Schwanenwik means Swan Bay, and people come here to feed the swans, coots, grebes, gray geese, seagulls and sundry other avians.

Pet Shop Boyz
Schmilinskystraße 15, 20099 St. Georg

Bei den Pet Shop Boyz möchte man sich auf der Stelle in einen Hund verwandeln und sich zu den Klängen von Hildegard Kneef durch die Auslagen fressen. Die Körbe voller Schweineohren, Schlund-Röhren und Pferdefell sind sicher nichts für Vegetarier, aber immerhin stinkt es nicht so wie in anderen Tierbedarfsläden. Für Hundebesitzerinnen, Katzenliebhaber, Vogelfreunde und Kleintierhalterinnen ist der Laden ein Traum, alle anderen überlegen sich, wie sie schnell auf den Hund kommen, um bei den Pet Shop Boyz einkaufen zu können.

Like Germany itself, this is not exactly a vegetarian's paradise: among the wares on display are baskets of pig's ears, snouts, and chewy rawhide. On the plus side, if you're a dog, cat, hamster or budgerigar owner, you'll find this friendly local pet store the perfect place to stock up on your day-to-day needs. And if you're not, you'll wish you were. **pet-shop-boyz.de**

Kaalia Street Cuisine
Rentzelstraße 13, 20146 Grindelviertel

Fast läuft man einfach dran vorbei, weil das Kaalia auf den ersten Blick wirkt wie einer der vielen Läden, wo man in der Nähe der Uni ein günstiges Mittagessen bekommt. Doch in der offenen Küche des kleinen, familiären Restaurants kocht Ulf Lindeholz etwas Besonderes: indische Gerichte mit französischem Einschlag und köstlicher Liebe zum raffinierten, hausgemachten Detail.

You could walk right by the place, because at first glance Kaalia looks like any of the numerous shops serving up cheap lunch fare near the university. But Ulf Lindenholz is cooking up something special in the open-plan kitchen of this small, informal restaurant: Indian cuisine with a French flair and a delectable love of sophisticated, homemade detail. **kaalia.de**

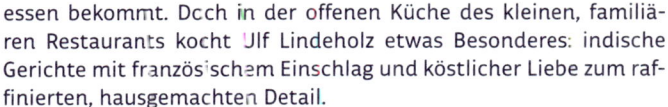

Lange Reihe 70, 20098 St. Georg

Mit einem schnöden „I-love-Hamburg"-Aufdruck kann ein Produkt im Kaufhaus Hamburg nicht landen, und auch wenn eine Designerin aus Paderborn gelungene Hamburg-Devotionalien entwirft, wird sie sie hier nicht anbieten können. Das Design muss schon anspruchsvoll sein und in Hamburg oder der unmittelbaren Umgebung hergestellt werden, damit es in den sorgfältig bestückten Regalen einen Platz findet.

If you're in search of tacky I-Love-Hamburg souvenirs stamped Made in China, don't come to Kaufhaus Hamburg. This department store sells everything you'd expect a department store to sell—but every item on its carefully stocked shelves is locally made and in immaculate taste. **kaufhaus-hamburg.de**

Paternoster

Grindelberg 62—66, 20144 Eimsbüttel

„Auf dem Dom müssten Sie dafür viel Geld bezahlen", aber im Bezirksamt Eimsbüttel kann man umsonst mit dem Karussell fahren. Der Paternoster rattert und knarzt elf Stockwerke hoch, und wenn man im letzten nicht aussteigt — Weiterfahrt ungefährlich —, kann man die überdimensionale Fahrradkette sehen, an der die 22 Kabinen hängen. Dann geht es wieder runter, aufrecht, nicht kopfüber, für eine Rundfahrt braucht der Umlauffahrstuhl fast fünf Minuten. Noch eine Runde? Nur keine Scheu, die Bezirksamtsmitarbeiter lassen sich von Fahrstuhltouristen nicht stören.

"You have to pay a lot of money at the Dom carnival for this." But in the Eimsbuettel district city government offices, a ride on the carousel is for free. The paternoster lift rattles and creaks its way up to the top story on the eleventh floor. And if you don't get out—don't worry, it's not dangerous — you get a glimpse of this

oversized bicycle chain studded with its 22 lifts compartments. Then back down you go, right side up, not upside down. The revolving elevator needs about five minutes to complete a round trip. Want to go another round? Don't be shy. District office employees are used to elevator tourists.

Bildwechsel
Kirchenallee 25, 20099 St. Georg

Vor lauter Handykameras und YouTube kann man sich kaum noch vorstellen, wie das war, als es in den 1970ern plötzlich Video gab und Film nicht mehr nur im Kino und im Fernsehen. In dieser Zeit legten ein paar Studentinnen der HfbK den Grundstein für Bildwechsel. Das Künstlerinnennetzwerk und -archiv ist bis heute selbstorganisiert und selbstfinanziert, unter anderem durch Veranstaltungen, die thematische Zusammenstellungen aus der über 7000 Videos und Filme umfassenden Kollektion präsentieren. Das Archiv ist mittwochs von 14 bis 19 Uhr geöffnet, es ist eine sehr gute Idee, sich vorher anzumelden: info@bildwechsel.org.

In the age of the handycam and YouTube, we've come a long way since the 1970s, when video technology became affordable and people began making their own movies instead of watching them on TV and at the cinema. That was when a group of students from Hamburg's Hochschule für Bildende Künste laid the foundations of what is now Bildwechsel, a self-funded video artists' collective and archive that holds events focusing on specific themes from its collection of over 7,000 films. The archive is open on Wednesdays from 2 to 7 pm, but it's a good idea to book first at info@bildwechsel.org.

bildwechsel.org

HAMBURGER BERGE

Hoch, hoch, hoch hinaus — Hamburg von oben
High, higher, highest—Hamburg from above

Köhlbrandbrücke
Weitsicht vom Wahrzeichen, 53 Meter
Spacious view from the city landmark, 53 meters
Dockland Van-der-Smissen-Straße 9
Beste Sicht von Deck, 25 Meter, 140 Stufen
Best view from the deck, 25 meters high, 140 steps
Aussichtsplattform des Planetariums Hindenburgstraße 1B
Hamburg von Norden, 42 Meter
Hamburg from the north, 42 meters
Himmelsleiter Elbchaussee
Himmlische Übersicht, 120 Stufen
Heavenly view, 120 steps
Turm des Mahnmals St. Nikolai Willy-Brandt-Straße 60
Mittendrin, mit Panoramafahrstuhl, 74 Meter
Smack in the middle, with panoramic elevator, 74 meters
Cafeteria 66 Grindelberg 66
Rundumsicht mit Bezirksbeamten, 12. Stock mit Paternoster
360° view, complete with city civil servants,
12th floor with paternoster lift
Energiebunker Neuhöfer Straße 7
Hamburg von Süden, 30 Meter *Hamburg from the south, 30 meters*
ViewPoint Grandeswerderstraße
Baustellenaufsicht, 13 Meter
Supervision of construction sites, 13 meters high
Altonaer Balkon Palmaille
Hafen, grün gerahmt, 27 Meter über der Elbe
The harbor framed in greenery, 27 meters above the Elbe

Schaugewächshäuser
Planten un Blomen, St. Pauli

Wenn Hamburg mal wieder scheußlich grau und ver-
regnet ist, bleibt nur die Flucht in die naheliegenden
Tropen. Gleich hinterm Dammtor in den Schauge-
wächshäusern des Botanischen Gartens in Planten un Blomen ist
es auch im Winter 25 Grad feucht-warm. Während der Regen auf das
Glasdach prasselt, wandelt man zwischen Farnen und Kakteen durch
die Klimazonen der Erde und träumt vom Hamburger Sommer.

*When Hamburg turns a dreary, rainy gray, the only op-
tion is escape to the nearby tropics. The forecast calls for a temperate
25 degrees Celsius—even in winter—in the greenhouses of the Planten un Blomen park's botanical garden just next to Dammtor train
station. The rain patters on the glass roof while you stroll among
the ferns and cacti through the earth's different climates and dream
about summer in Hamburg.* **plantenunblomen.hamburg.de**

Schaukeln an der Alster
Eduard-Rhein-Ufer, 22087 Uhlenhorst

Darf ich auch mal? Bitte! Nur ganz, ganz kurz! Eigentlich dürfen auf dem Spielplatz neben dem Café
Alsterperle natürlich nur die Kinder mit den Augen
auf die Alster in den Himmel schaukeln. Aber die Gelegenheit ist
auch für Erwachsene einfach zu verlockend, um sie ungenutzt ver-
streichen zu lassen.

*Can I have a turn? Please! Just for a sec! Actually, of
course, the swing set on the playground adjacent to the Alsterperle
café is reserved for children to swing skyward as they gaze out over
the Alster, but grownups likewise find it too tempting to pass up.*

Abaton Kino
Allende-Platz 3, 20146 Rotherbaum

Rote Samtsessel, eine Bar im Foyer und ausgesuchte Filme — das Abaton strahlt genau das aus,
was man sich unter einem guten Programmkino
vorstellt. Und das nicht zufällig, denn es war in den 1970er Jahren
das erste Programmkino in Deutschland, oder besser gesagt, durch
das inzwischen vielfach ausgezeichnete Filmangebot des Abatons
mit vielen untertitelten Originalfassungen und Erstaufführungen
mit Filmemachern und Gästen wurde der Begriff Programmkino
überhaupt erst geprägt. Heute ist das Abaton eine Institution.

*Red velvet seats, a bar in the lobby and first-rate films:
The Abaton offers exactly what you would expect from a good art
cinema. And that is not just a coincidence. The Abaton was the first
of its kind in Germany, dating back to the 1970s. In fact, the Abaton
really coined the term art house cinema through its award-winning
film program, many shown in original language versions with sub-
titles, as well as world premières with filmmakers and special guests
in attendance. Abaton is today a real institution.* **abaton.de**

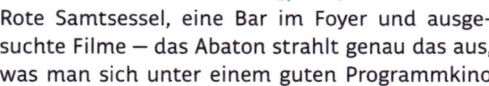

Anleger am Uhlenhorster Fährhaus
Schöne Aussicht, 22085 Uhlenhorst

Vom Jungfernstieg kommend legen die Linienschiffe
der Alster-Touristik hier tagsüber stündlich an, bevor
sie nach Winterhude weiterschippern. Wenn die unter-
gehende Sonne die Innenstadt abends orange beleuchtet und die
ruhige Alster pfirsichfarben schimmert, kann man im Halbdunkeln
auf dem Anleger sitzen und versuchen, die vorbeischwimmenden
Wasservögel an ihren Umrissen zu erkennen, während man den Ge-
sprächen der Leute auf den anderen Bänken lauscht.

*During the day, Alster-Touristik's cruise boats stop here
every hour on their way from Jungfernstieg to Winterhude. At sunset,*

*when the city lights up in orange and the calm waters of the Alster
take on a peach-colored shimmer, there's nothing nicer to sit on a
quayside bench, watch the water birds, and eavesdrop on your neigh-
bors' conversations.*

Hadley's Café Bar
Beim Schlump 84 A, 20144 Eimsbüttel

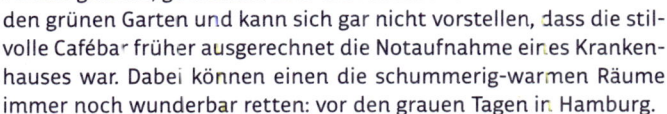

Oben in der Galerie des Hadley's in die großen
Polster gelehnt, guckt man über die Terrasse in
den grünen Garten und kann sich gar nicht vorstellen, dass die stil-
volle Cafébar früher ausgerechnet die Notaufnahme eines Kranken-
hauses war. Dabei können einen die schummerig-warmen Räume
immer noch wunderbar retten: vor den grauen Tagen in Hamburg.

*There you sit in a big, comfortable armchair in Hadley's
mezzanine, looking across the terrace to the lovely green garden.
Hard to imagine that this stylish café and bar was once a hospital
emergency room. But one of the bar's cozy rooms with chiaroscuro
lighting can still be a real lifesaver—from the gray weather in Hamburg.* hadleys.de

Mutterland
Ernst-Merck-Straße 9-11, 20099 St. Georg

Fast wie von Muttern: Slowfood-Marmeladen und
handgemachte Pralinen, hausgemachte Kuchen
zum eigenen Kaffee und altmodische Bonbons.
Die heimischen Delikatessen bei Mutterland stammen aus kleinen,
familiengeführten Manufakturen und sind so hübsch verpackt und
präsentiert, dass die drei Läden am Hauptbahnhof, in Eppendorf
und in der Altstadt dafür sogar schon Preise gewonnen haben.

*Almost like mom's: slow-food jams and handmade pra-
lines, homemade cakes to go with their own coffee, and old-fashio-
ned candies and sweets. The domestic delicacies at Mutterland are*

sourced from small, family-run manufacturers and are so prettily packaged and presented that the three stores—at the main station, in Eppendorf and Altstadt—have received numerous industry accolades. **mutterland.de**

Cafeteria 66 in den Grindelhochhäusern
Grindelberg 66, 20144 Eimsbüttel

Die Cafeteria 66 ist im Grunde die Kantine des Bezirksamts Eimsbüttel. Für 36 Cent Aufschlag können auch „Nichtbedienstete" dort zu Mittag essen und den Verwaltungsfachgesprächen der Angestellten lauschen. Aber das ist nicht der Punkt. Der Punkt ist der Rundumblick über Hamburg vom 12. Stock eines der denkmalgeschützten ersten Wohnhochhäuser Deutschlands. Wen interessiert da schon noch der Erbseneintopf?

Cafeteria 66 is actually the employee cafeteria for the Eimsbüttel district city government offices. But for a 36 cents surcharge, anyone who is not a civil servant can also have lunch and eavesdrop on the conversations about city administration issues. But that's not the point. The big draw is the panoramic view of Hamburg from the 12th floor of one of Germany's first high-rise residential buildings, now a listed historic building. Who's even still interested in the vegetable stew? **cafeteria66.de**

Pappenheimer Wirtschaft
Papenhuder Straße 26, 22087 Uhlenhorst

Wenn man von der norddeutschen Küche mal die Nase voll hat, ist die Pappenheimer Wirtschaft eine echte Alternative, denn hier ist alles ganz anders, und zwar fränkisch: Aus Nürnberg importierte Wurstvariationen, Schäufele, Spätzle und Topfenpalatschinken, dazu Landbrot mit Fenchel, Anis, Koriander und Kümmel, außerdem ausgewählte Weine, Landbiere und Schnäpse. Lecker!

If you've had your fill of north German cuisine, Pappenheimer Wirtschaft is a real alternative, serving up an entirely different menu hailing from the south in Franconia: sausages imported from Nuremberg, pork shoulder, Spätzle noodles, Topfenpalatschinken crepes with sweet white cheese, rustic bread flavored with fennel, anise, coriander and cumin, as well as select wines, beers and various schnapps. Yummy! pappenheimer-wirtschaft.de

Café Leonar
Grindelhof 59, 20146 Rotherbaum

Um die Ecke von der Uni, im ehemaligen jüdischen Viertel am Grindel, gibt es seit einigen Jahren wieder ein jüdisches Kaffeehaus. Die Küche ist kosher und jüdisch-international, die hausgemachten Kuchen sind grandios. Wann immer möglich sollte man den Besuch des Cafés mit der Teilnahme an einer Veranstaltung im angeschlossenen Jüdischen Salon verbinden, der mit einer großen Bandbreite an Veranstaltungen der jüdischen Kultur in Hamburg Raum gibt.

The old Jewish neighborhood Grindel is now again home to a Jewish café located just around the corner from the university. The kitchen cooks kosher and serves Jewish-international dishes. The homemade cakes are marvelous. And if you are lucky, they might be holding an event in the adjacent Jewish Salon, which offers a wide-ranging program on Jewish culture in Hamburg. cafeleonar.de

Café Gnosa
Lange Reihe 93, 20099 St. Georg

Im Café Gnosa kristallisiert sich das Prinzip des Regenbogen-Laufstegs Lange Reihe bei hausgemachter Torte oder Sektchen: sehen und gesehen werden. Das alteingesessene, plüschige Kaffeehaus ist weit über seine schwul-lesbische

Stammkundschaft hinaus beliebt, und gerade am Sonntag sind Sitzplätze knapp und begehrt. Die Betreiber schätzen die Gewohnheiten ihrer Gäste realistisch ein und servieren Frühstück bis vier Uhr nachmittags.

Lange Reihe is one of Hamburg's most popular gay haunts, and Café Gnosa is the place to see and be seen. This cozy and long-established coffee house, popular with gays and straights alike, specializes in homemade Torte and chilled Sekt. Seating can be in short supply on Sundays. In a pragmatic acceptance of their customers' nightowl lifestyles, the owners serve breakfast until 4 pm. **gnosa.de**

Zoologisches Museum
Martin-Luther-King-Platz 3,
20146 Eimsbüttel

Alles, was schlimm ist, ist irgendwie auch faszinierend. Bei einem Besuch im Zoologischen Museum der Uni Hamburg muss man so einiges ausblenden, nämlich dass die Tiere tot sind und die Ursprünge des Museums in den „hanseatischen Seefahrer- und Entdeckertraditionen vor allem des 19. Jahrhunderts" liegen, sprich: in der Kolonialzeit. Wenn das gelingt, ist es allerdings spannend, auf 2000 Quadratmetern Tiere (zumindest als Präparate) ganz aus der Nähe betrachten zu können, unter anderem Antje von Hagenbeck, das beliebte NDR-Walross.

Somehow bad things can be fascinating. A visit to the Zoological Museum of the University of Hamburg requires that you suppress certain unpleasant facts—namely that the animals on display are dead, and that the museum's origins are "tightly interwoven with the traditions of Hanseatic sailors and explorers particularly of the 19th century," in other words the colonial period. If you can do that, however, you'll be fascinated to explore the 2,000-square-meter exhibition space and see the animals (or at least life-like specimens thereof) up close, including Hagenbeck Tierpark's Antje, the much-loved mascot of public broadcaster NDR. **uni-hamburg.de**

HAMBURGER
OSTEN →

Oldtimer Tankstelle Brandshof
Billhorner Röhrendamm 4,
20539 Rothenburgsort

Als Alex Piatschek und Jann de Boer 2011 ihre Oldtimer-Tankstelle eröffneten, überschlug sich die Presse fast vor Begeisterung. Es ist aber auch wirklich beeindruckend, wie sie die denkmalgeschützte Tankstelle von 1953 originalgetreu restauriert haben und sie nun mit Leben füllen: Neben der GTÜ-Prüfstation ist ab vier Uhr morgens der stilechte Erfrischungsraum geöffnet, und am Wochenende fahren die Oldtimer vor zum Offenen Treffen für Altes Blech.

Alex Piatschek and Jann de Boer attracted big-time media attention when they opened their vintage petrol station in 2011. Dating from 1953, it's now a listed building that has been authentically restored and brought back to life as a vehicle inspection station. There's also a café that opens at 4 am, and a historic car rally each weekend. **tankstelle-brandshof.de**

Adeola Afro Bistro
Wandsbeker Chaussee 47, 22089 Wandsbek

Im Adeola Afro Bistro in einer 50er-Jahre-Ladenzeile in der Wandsbeker Chaussee ist das Ambiente so familiär und herzlich, als sei man bei Helen Hilbel im Wohnzimmer. Ihre Küche befindet sich direkt im Gastraum, und die Inhaberin kocht selbst: Kochbananen, Jollof Reis, gebratener Fisch — das nigerianische Essen kommt in großen Portionen und ist in der scharfen Version genau richtig.

So welcoming is this Nigerian bistro, located in a row of 1950s shops on Wandsbeker Chaussee, that you'll think you've wandered into owner Helen Hilbel's living room by mistake. The kitchen is actually in the dining area, and Helen does the cooking herself: generous helpings of plantain, jollof rice and fried fish, with just the right degree of spiciness. **afro-bistro.de**

Seumestraße 10, 22089 Wandsbek

„Bier ist für alle da!", sagt Esther Isaak de Schmidt-Bohländer und die muss es wissen, denn sie empfiehlt den Kundinnen und Kunden ihres Bierlands das passende Bier auf den Leib. 200 Sorten stehen in dem Fachgeschäft zur Auswahl, und die Inhaberin scheint sie wirklich alle zu kennen. Sie ist außerdem eine der Gründerinnen der deutschen Barley's Angels, einer Vereinigung aus den USA, die Bierkultur unter Frauen fördern will und den Brauereien klarmachen, dass sie Frauen ihre Sixpacks nicht im pinkfarbenen Handtaschenlook anzubieten brauchen. Cheers!

Owner Esther Isaak de Schmidt-Böhlander says there's a beer to suit every taste—and she should know, since she stocks around two hundred. She appears to be an expert on all of them, and will happily recommend one that's right for you. Esther also co-founded the German branch of Barley's Angels, a US organization of women who are passionate about beer, and which advises brewers on marketing to women. We'll drink to that! bierland-hamburg.de

Hamburger Sternwarte

Gojenbergsweg 112, 21029 Bergedorf

Auch wenn sie inzwischen zur Uni Hamburg gehört und Studentinnen und Studenten der Astrophysik sich hier Vorträge mit Titeln wie „Hot topics in solar plasma physics" anhören — die Hamburger Sternwarte ist alles andere als ein Elfenbeinturm. Zwar wird in den Kuppelbauten von 1912 bis heute astronomische Grundlagenforschung betrieben, aber das denkmalgeschützte Gelände steht Besuchern bei vielen Veranstaltungen offen, und einmal im Monat darf man im Rahmen einer Führung sogar selbst an die riesigen Teleskope treten und mal so richtig Sterne sehen.

The domed observatory now belongs to Hamburg University. It has been carrying out fundamental research since 1912, and holds lectures for astrophysics students with titles like Hot Topics in Solar Plasma Physics. But this listed building is anything but an ivory tower, and there are lots of public events, including monthly tours in which you can try your hand at stargazing through the huge telescopes. **hs.uni-hamburg.de**

Café Brooks
Hasselbrookstraße 37, 22089 Eilbek

Man muss schon in der Nachbarschaft wohnen oder genau wissen, wo in Hasselbrook das schöne Café Brooks ist, sonst kommt man dort vielleicht nie vorbei und verpasst — alles: die schlichte, aber durchkomponierte Einrichtung, den köstlichen, selbstgemachten Kuchen, die Sonne an Tischen unter Bäumen und die nette Bande von Freunden, die das Café betreibt.

You have to live in the Hasselbrook or know exactly where to find the lovely Café Brooks. Otherwise, you might never pass by and you'd miss it all—the simple but stylish interior, the delicious homemade cakes, the sunny tables under the trees and the nice bunch of friends who run the café. **cafebrooks.de**

Mode Schneider
Caspar-Voght-Straße 94, 20535 Eilbek

Mode Schneider ist eines der Modegeschäfte alter Schule, deren Angebot absolut unhip ist. Aber zwischen den langen Nachthemden mit Leopardendruck oder Streublumendekor, den Stretchhosen und Strickpullovern mit Zopfmuster, zwischen Bettwäsche, Handtüchern, Wolle und Garn findet man doch das ein oder andere schöne Oberteil und schlichte, klassische Unterwäsche für wirklich wenig Geld.

An old-school clothing store packed with totally unhip creations like long leopard- and flower-print nightshirts, stretch pants and knitted pullovers with braided patterns, and with bed linen, towels, wool and yarn. But there's no shortage of bargains, and every chance of finding a really stylish top or some simple, classic underwear.

113

Bergedorfer Schifffahrtslinie
Serrahnstraße 1, 21029 Bergedorf

Um mal was ganz anderes zu sehen, kann man mit der S-Bahn nach Bergedorf rausfahren und von dort mit einer der Barkassen der Bergedorfer Schifffahrtslinie Richtung Hafencity zurückschippern. Die Barkassen fahren jenseits der Elbbrücken die Dove Elbe runter, durch die idyllischen Vierlande und den industriellen Hamburger Osten, dort entlang, wo die Schiffe der gewöhnlichen Hafenrundfahrten sich selten hinwagen.

For a very different view of Hamburg, take the S-Bahn to Bergedorf and then head back towards Hafencity on a launch operated by Bergedorfer Schifffahrtslinie. This will take you down the Dove Elbe beyond the Elbe bridges, through the idyllic Vierlande district and Hamburg's industrial east, showing you places you won't see on the usual harbor cruises. **barkassenfahrt.de**

Boberger Düne und See
Billwerder Billdeich, 22113 Lohbrügge

Ja, ja, ja, die steht wirklich in jedem Reiseführer, die Boberger Düne. Aber trotzdem, ohne einen Hinweis auf diese letzte Wanderdüne Hamburgs und das dazugehörige Naturschutzgebiet mit See würde einfach etwas fehlen. So schön natürlich wie in diesem ehemaligen Baggersee mit Sandstrand kann man sich sonst kaum irgendwo in Hamburg erfrischen und entspannen.

Yes, we know the Boberger Dunes are in every Hamburg travel guide, but we can't go without mentioning them. They're the city's last remaining dunes that you can walk in, and there's also a nature reserve, a dredged lake and a sandy beach. There's no better place in Hamburg to relax and get a breath of fresh air.

Schn€ppchen Gebrauchtwaren-Paradies
Wandsbeker Chaussee 189, 22089 Wandsbek

„Schn€ppi" das Krokodil ist knallpink und schreibt sich mit einem Eurozeichen statt einem „e" — zugegeben, das Schn€ppchen Gebrauchtwaren-Paradies wirkt erst mal ziemlich trashig. Aber Name und Eurozeichen sind Programm, denn hier gibt es Anrichten aus Wurzelholz oder stilechte Kommödchen wirklich als Schäppchen. Und weil der Laden das andere Ende einer Firma für Haushaltsauflösungen ist, gibt es auch sonst alles — bis hin zum angebrochenen Putzmittel.

The crocodile "Schn€ppi" is bright pink and spells her name with a euro sign instead of the letter 'e,' OK, the Schn€ppchen second-hand paradise makes a trashy first impression. But the name and the euro sign are really what it's all about: sideboards in burl wood or designer chest of drawers for very little money. And the store also doubles as a business for clearing out households. It has every-thing—even half-used bottles of cleaning products.

schneppchen-paradies.de

Bunkermuseum
Wichernsweg 16, 20537 Hamm

Nein, man kann sich nicht vorstellen, wie das war, wenn sich im Zweiten Weltkrieg mehrere Hundert Menschen stehend in den vier niedrigen Röhren des unter-irdischen Bunkers in Hamm quetschten, während über ihren Köp-fen stundenlang die Bomben niedergingen und explodierten. Aber wenn während einer der Führungen durch das heutige Bunkermuseum das Licht ausgeht und in der stockdunklen Enge historische Tonaufnahmen eingespielt werden, bekommt man doch eine vage Ahnung davon.

During the second world war, several hundred people would take refuge from the falling bombs in the four low-roofed tunnels of this air-raid shelter in Hamm. It's hard to imagine what a claustrophobic ordeal this must have been, but a guided tour of the Bunkermuseum will give you an idea: during the tour, you'll hear wartime recordings of the bombing played in pitch darkness.
hh-hamm.de/bunkermuseum

117

Der Mobile Fahrradladen
In den Saal 3, 22159 Berne und überall

Zum Radfahren hat Felix Viole selbst kaum noch Zeit, denn vor ein paar Jahren hatte der Fahrradmechaniker eine echt gute Idee: den Mobilen Fahrradladen. Mit seiner Werkstatt hinten im Kastenwagen ist er überall dort im Einsatz, wo es kaputte Fahrräder gibt: bei seinen Kunden zu Hause, bei der Arbeit oder auch bei echten Notfällen unterwegs. Seinen kompetenten Service bietet er von morgens um sechs bis spät abends an, wenn andere Fahrradläden schon längst Feierabend haben — und er ist ein echt netter Typ.

Bike mechanic Felix Viole has little time for cycling these days: a few years ago, he had the bright idea of setting up a mobile bike shop in the back of his van. He'll go anywhere there are broken bicycles to be fixed, whether it be his customers' homes and workplaces, or out on the road. Felix works from 6 am to late in the evening, long after most conventional bike shops have closed—and he's a really nice guy into the bargain. **mobiler-fahrradladen.de**

NORD
NORD
WEST

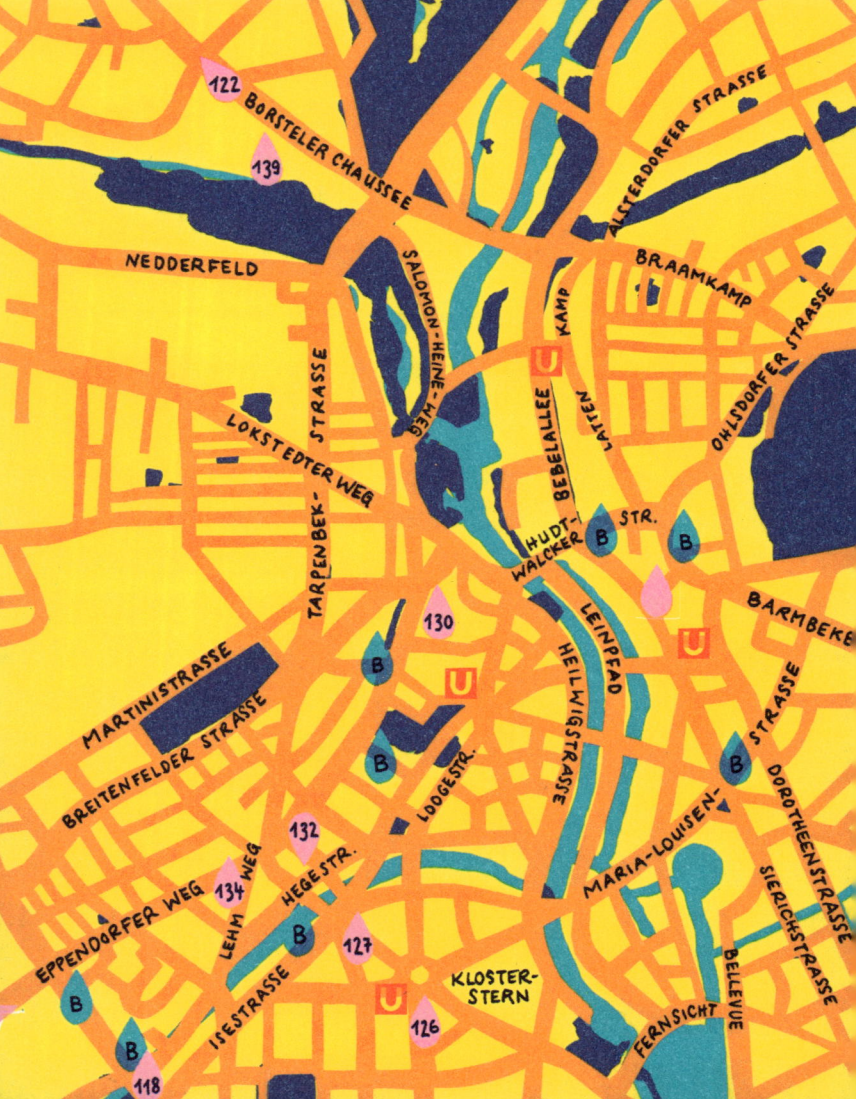

Ist man sonst nur St. Pauli gewohnt, fällt einem beim sonntäglichen Besuch im Balz & Balz erstmal das hohe Aufkommen von Perlenohrsteckern auf. Doch was zählen Vorurteile gegenüber Eppendorf und seinen Bewohnerinnen, wenn das Frühstück köstlich ist, der Kaffee hervorragend, das Ambiente schlicht und hochwertig – und die Leute so nett?

Anyone not accustomed to venturing beyond the borders of St. Pauli will be struck by the sheer number of pearl stud earrings confronting them when they walk into Balz & Balz on a Sunday. But what do preconceived notions about Eppendorf and its inhabitants matter when the breakfast is delicious, the coffee outstanding, the atmosphere understated and upscale—and the people are so nice?
balzundbalz.de

Als sie in den späten 1950er Jahren als „Bürostadt im Grünen" erdacht wurde, sollte die City Nord die historische Innenstadt entlasten und gleichzeitig die Zentralen großer Unternehmen in Hamburg halten. Auf den ersten Blick sieht die City Nord aus wie ein hässliches Relikt der 1970er, aber bei einem Spaziergang mit einem Architekturführer in der Hand gelangt man schnell zu komplexeren Ansichten über die bizarre Schönheit dieser „Modellstadt der Moderne", in der bis heute fast 30 000 Menschen arbeiten.

The vast office blocks and parklands of City Nord were first conceived in the late 1950s, in an effort to relieve the pressure on the historic city center and encourage corporations to maintain their headquarters in Hamburg. Today, the area looks like a depressing 1970s relic, but a stroll with an architectural guidebook gives a more nuanced picture of this modernist and strangely beautiful model city, still the workplace of nearly 30,000 people. **city-nord.org**

Kafayas Café & Spécialités
Semperstraße 64, 22303 Barmbek

In einer Seitenstraße unter Bäumen wird man bei Kafayas mit der großen Auswahl an Tartes konfrontiert und kann sich gar nicht entscheiden — Schoko-Karamell-Marshmellow oder Weiße Trüffel mit Himbeeren? Alle sehen so köstlich aus und feist. Wer auf die Tarte-Frage keine Antwort findet, sollte das locker-leichte Frühstücksomelett probieren.

On corner of a treelined side street, Kafayas presents you with some tough choices. Take the mouthwatering array of tarts, for example: do you go for chocolate, caramel and marshmallow, or white truffle with raspberries? For the less sweet of tooth, the light, fluffy breakfast omelet makes the perfect start to the day. **kafayas.de**

Ohlsdorfer Friedhof
Fuhlsbüttler Straße 756, 22337 Ohlsdorf

Der Friedhof Ohlsdorf vereint auf sich gleich mehrere Superlative: Er ist nicht nur der größte Parkfriedhof der Welt, sondern auch Hamburgs größte Grünanlage. Er ist so groß, dass er 17 Kilometer eigene Straßen hat und außerdem 25 Bushaltestellen. Auf dem Friedhof kann man die Gräber berühmter Hamburger suchen, so manche Skulptur bewundern oder sich einfach zwischen Rhododendron naherholen.

Ohlsdorf Cemetery is a place of superlatives: not only is it the largest park cemetery in the world, but also Hamburg's biggest green space. It is so big that some 11 miles of roads with 25 bus stops cut through it, inviting you to seek out the graves of prominent Hamburg citizens, admire some of the sculptures or simply take a stroll among the rhododendrons. **friedhof-hamburg.de/ohlsdorf**

122

Niendorfer Gehege
Niendorfer Gehege, 22453 Niendorf

Also mit Menschen hat das Damwild im Niendorfer Gehege nun wirklich kein Problem. Besucher am Zaun? Sicher kein Grund zum Weglaufen. Denn die Rehe und Hirsche stehen ja regelmäßig Aug' in Aug' mit Spaziergängern, die sie interessiert beim Äsen beobachten, bei Hirschkämpfen mitfiebern oder sie einfach ergriffen bewundern — „Sind die süüüß!"

The deer in the Niendorfer Wildgehege deer park really have no problem with people. Passersby at the fence? That is certainly no reason to run away. The deer and bucks are used to the hikers watching them graze. Or the cheers for the battling bucks. Or the constant crooning: "Aren't they cuuuute!"

123

Hamburger Biergarten
Hindenburgstraße 2, 22303 Barmbek

Inzwischen gibt es in Hamburg so einige Biergärten nach bayerischem Vorbild, aber wirklich klassische Biergartenatmosphäre bietet eigentlich nur der „Hamburger Biergarten" beim Landhaus Walter. Über den langen Bierbänken unterm Blätterdach baumeln die Glühbirnengirlanden im Abendwind, und wenn es dämmert, wird der Garten von der blauen Bretterbude erleuchtet, wo sich für Würste, Brez'n, Bier und am „Kassenhaus" getrennte Schlangen bilden.

Meanwhile Hamburg is home to a good handful of Bavarian-style beer gardens. But the truly classic beer garden atmosphere can only be found at the Hamburger Biergarten at Landhaus Walter. The garlands of light bulbs sway in the evening wind under the canopy of leaves. And come sunset, the blue shack serving the food and drinks illuminates the garden. Two lines form in typical beer garden style, one for ordering sausages, pretzels and beer and the other in front of the "Cash House" to pay for it all. landhauswalter.de

Planespotting auf dem Affenfelsen
Holtkoppel 100, 22415 Fuhlsbüttel

Auf dem Affenfelsen lauern die Männer mit Objektiven so groß wie Kanonenrohre. Sie warten auf Flugzeuge, die hier, direkt neben der Landebahn, unheimlich nah passieren. Es macht Spaß, sich mal unter die „Planespotter" zu mischen, auch wenn man ihren sportlichen Ehrgeiz, so viele Flieger wie möglich zu fotografieren, nicht teilt. Nur eins bitte nicht: dabei summen „Wind Nord-Ost, Startbahn null drei ..."

The Affenfelsen, or Monkey Rock, provides a convenient vantage point for hordes of male planespotters armed with bazooka-sized camera lenses. Even if you don't share their enthusiasm for picture taking, they provide almost as much entertainment as the planes themselves, which land at unnervingly close range.

Kältekammer bei Globetrotter
Wiesendamm 1, 22305 Barmbek

Die eine Wand ist aus Glas, und alle, die vorbeigehen, grinsen, während man drinnen auf Eisblöcken hockt wie in einem tiefgefrorenen Aquarium. Es ist aber auch ziemlich cool, dass man in der Kältekammer bei Globetrotter die angebotene Funktionskleidung gleich mal auf ihre Funktionalität testen kann. Und siehe da, die Outdoor-Jacke ist auch nach 15 Minuten bei minus zehn Grad noch mummelig warm.

Outdoor clothing and equipment retailer Globetrotter has a refrigerated room, strewn with blocks of ice, where customers can try out products at temperatures of minus 10 degrees Celsius. One of the walls is made of glass, creating a deep-frozen aquarium that provides free entertainment for grinning passers-by.

globetrotter.de

AM WASSER GEBAUT

Kupfer, Putz & Klinker — Hamburger Architektur
Copper, plaster and brick—Hamburg architecture

Hamburg Süd International Style in Hamburg
international style
Stellahaus Expressionismus in hellblau
expressionism in light blue
Krematorium Ohlsdorf Schumachers letzter Bau
Schumacher's last building
Chilehaus Hamburgs stolzes Klinkerschiff
Hamburg's proud brick boat
Bürohaus Steckelhörn 11, Rückseite 1,3 Meter Baulücke, neu gefüllt
Office building Steckelhörn 11, back side
1.3 meters vacant lot, filled in
Dulsberg-Siedlung Rote Siedlung im Grünen
red-brick residential area on the city's green outskirts
City Nord Schön und brutal
beautiful and brutal
Grindel-Hochhäuser Gelbe Scheiben, schön geschnitten
yellow blocks, slick shapes
Dockland Schnellboot mit Terrasse
speedboat with terrace
Hammer Kirche Hammernachkriegsbau
remarkable post-war architecture
Jenisch Haus Weißer Würfel im Park
white cube in the park

U-Bahn-Station Klosterstern
Klosterstern, 20149 Eppendorf

Von der Rothenbaumchaussee kommend unterm Kupferdach mit dem blau-weißen HOCHBAHN-Schriftzug die Treppe runter, durch die holzbraunen Schwingtüren in die U-Bahn-Station Klosterstern. Vorbei an messinggefassten Schaukästen und hellblau-beige-braunen Wandfliesen, auf abschüssigem Grund über die zweite Treppe auf den Bahnsteig, der sich im Licht der Kette dreieckiger Deckenleuchten in eine Kurve schmiegt, Platz nehmen auf einer hölzernen Bank, die glatt poliert ist von wartenden Händen und Hintern seit 1929.

Head down the steps beneath the copper roof and blue-and-white HOCHBAHN sign on Rothenbaumchaussee, and go through the brown wooden swing doors into Klosterstern U-Bahn station. Then take the second steep flight of stairs past the brass-framed display cases and blue, beige and brown tiled wall to the curving platform with its string of triangular ceiling lights. The seats where you wait for your train date from 1929, and have been worn smooth by countless travelers. **hamburger-untergrundbahn.de**

Kaufrausch
Isestraße 74, 20149 Eppendorf

Aus Harry's Bar gleich beim Eingang duftet es nach Espresso. Ledertaschen, Haarschmuck und Dessous locken die Treppe hoch durch die verwinkelte Ladengalerie, die sich sieben Boutiquen seit über dreißig Jahren teilen. Françoise Henrichs ist von Anfang an dabei, in ihrem Laden auf dem ersten Treppenabsatz gibt es wunderbar überdrehte Unikate der englischen Porzellangestalterin Mary Rose Young, Küchenspielzeug für Erwachsene von Pylones und extrem belastbare Loqi-Shopper, in die man alles gleich einpacken kann, wenn einen der Kaufrausch überfällt.

The enticing aroma of espresso wafting from Harry's Bar greets you as soon as you walk in the door. Leather bags, hair accessories and lingerie lure you up the stairs through the labyrinth gallery shop, the shared space of seven boutiques for over thirty years now. Françoise Henrichs was there from the start. Her shop on the first landing has wonderful one-of-a-kind whimsical English porcelain pieces from designer Mary Rose Young; kitchen toys for adults from Pylones; and extremely durable shopping bags, which you can use right away to pack up whatever you get on your Kaufrausch—German for shopping spree. **kaufrausch-hamburg.de**

128

Schön & ehrlich
Gertigstraße 18, 22303 Winterhude

Der ganze Laden ist so wie sein Angebot: schön, hell, puristisch. Designerlampen und Betonschalen, Alphabetbeutel und Letterpress-Papeterie, Bilder, Bücher, Becher — der Name „schön & ehrlich" ist gut gewählt, denn die handverlesenen Produkte kleiner Designlabels und die selbstgefertigten Einzelstücke, die Indra Tausendschön und Christina Torbahn in ihrer eigenen Manufaktur auf Wunsch auch personalisieren, sind sehr schön, ehrlich.

The whole store is like its merchandise: beautiful, bright, purist. And the name "schön & ehrlich" is a good fit because everything here is really beautiful and honest: designer lamps and concrete bowls, alphabet bags and letterpress stationary, pictures, books, mugs. All products are from small designer labels or the workshop of the owners, who will customize their one-of-a-kind pieces on request. **schoen-und-ehrlich.de**

Hörkonzerte vor der Freilichtbühne
Jahnring 71, 22303 Barmbek

Das Konzertprogramm der Freilichtbühne im Stadtpark sollte man ganz genau im Auge behalten, denn bei schönem Wetter kann man die Musik auch ohne Eintrittskarte genießen. Zwar ist wegen der dichten Hecken rund um das Bühnengelände nichts von der Show zu sehen, aber dafür kann man das gesparte Geld in einen guten Wein oder ein geselliges Grillpicknick investieren und statt vor der Bühne zu stehen gemütlich an selbst mitgebrachten Tischen und Stühlen sitzen.

Those of a cheapskate turn of mind can enjoy the outdoor concert program at the Stadtpark without paying to get in. You won't actually see anything, thanks to the dense hedges around the auditorium, but who cares? Spend the ticket money on a picnic and a bottle or two of wine, bring a folding chair, and treat your ears to some seriously good music. open-r.de

Otto F. K. Koch
Eppendorfer Landstraße 104,
20249 Eppendorf

Mit hanseatischem Understatement firmiert Otto F. K. Koch schlicht als „Papeterie". Dabei bietet das über einhundert Jahre alte Traditionsgeschäft wesentlich mehr, denn eigentlich stecken hier mehrere Läden unter einem Dach: ein Fachsortiment mit Bürobedarf im Keller, vorne im Laden alltägliche und edle Papeterie, Bastel-, Künstler- und Schulbedarf in der Mitte und in den Tiefen des Geschäfts ein ganzer Spielwarenladen mit ausgezeichnetem Brettspielsortiment. Klassischer Einzelhandel ganz wie er sein soll, freundliche Beratung inklusive.

In typical Hanseatic understatement, Otto F. K. Koch simply calls itself a "Papeterie." But this tradition-rich store, in business

for over a century, offers so much more. It actually houses several shops under one roof: a specialized office supply in the basement, fine stationary up at the entrance, arts, craft and school supplies in the middle and way in the back, a whole toy store with an excellent board game selection. A classic small retail store, just as it should be—friendly service included. **papeterie-hamburg.de**

131

Die Wäscherei
Mexikoring 27–29, 22297 City Nord

Viele Wohnungen (und vielleicht die ganze Welt) wären wesentlich schöner, wenn alle in der Wäscherei einkaufen würden und nicht bei IKEA. Das Angebot auf den endlosen Etagen des „Lifestylehauses" in der City Nord ist absolut überwältigend, es gibt alles von Ethnokitsch-Wohnaccessoires über Mode bis hin zu Designermöbeln in allen möglichen Stilen und aus Materialien, die man alle anfassen möchte, weil sie so schön aussehen.

The world would be a far better looking place if everyone furnished their houses not from IKEA, but from Die Wäscherei ("The Laundry"). This "lifestyle store" in City Nord offers floor after floor of everything from kitsch ethnic accessories to fashion clothing and designer furniture so goodlooking you'll want to kiss it.
die-waescherei.de

132

Kunstgenuss
Hegestieg 14, 20249 Eppendorf

Hamburgs größte Auswahl an Wandkalendern wird hier im Souterrain eines Jugendstil-Hauses in Eppendorf nicht etwa wie üblich auf einer Art Kleiderstange präsentiert, sondern frontal und dicht an dicht — in „Petersburger Hängung". Das erleichtert die Auswahl und das Blättern ungemein und ist ein platzökonomisches Kunststück ebenso wie die Präsentation der insgesamt 7000

Postkarten, 2500 davon Kunstkarten mit Motiven von der Antike bis heute, die die übrigen Wände des Ladens bedecken.

The basement of this Art Nouveau building in Eppendorf houses Hamburg's largest selection of wall calendars. They are not displayed on the usual boring racks, but face forward, one next to the other, and tightly packed, in the so-called salon hang style, like in old museums. This makes it so much easier to choose, as well as being a space-saving art work itself. So is the display of more than 7,000 postcards covering the store's other walls, 2,500 of which are art cards with motifs from antiquity to contemporary art.

kunstgenuss-hamburg.de

Gräber Räder
Fuhlsbüttler Straße 269, 22307 Barmbek

133

Bei Gräber Räder heißen Fahrräder noch Fahrräder und nicht etwa Bikes, und niemand wird herablassend behandelt, nur weil er sich nicht richtig auskennt. Ganz im Gegenteil, Norbert, Jens und Manfred beraten gern und ausführlich, zum Beispiel wenn man noch nicht sicher ist, welches der Touren- und Cityräder infrage kommt, welcher Brooks-Sattel der richtige ist oder ob die Laufräder neu zentriert werden müssen.

At Gräber Räder, a two-wheeled mode of transportation with a bell on the handlebars is called a Fahrrad, not a bike. Unpretentious owner Norbert Gräber and his crew, Jens and Manfred, eschew the English word, but are generous with advice on whether to buy a touring or city bike, which saddle is right for you, and how to rebalance your wheels. **graeber-raeder.de**

134

Alles was skandinavisch ist, steht in Hamburg hoch im Kurs. Liegt es daran, dass Teile des heutigen Hamburgs lange unter dänischer Verwaltung standen? Oder daran, dass sich die norddeutsche und die skandinavische Lebensart sowieso ziemlich ähnlich sind? Im minimalistischen Café der dänischen Brüder Lund kann man über diese Fragen bei einem guten Cappuccino und einem Sandwich sinnieren.

Why is it that Hamburg is crazy about all things Scandinavian? Is it because parts of what is today Hamburg were for many years under Danish administration, or is it perhaps due to the fact that the lifestyles of northern Germany and the Nordics are anyway fairly similar? You can mull these and other considerations over a good cappuccino and a sandwich at this minimalist café run by the Danish Lund brothers.

135

Das „Zentrum für Schönere Künste" in den weitläufigen Hallen der ehemaligen Maschinenfabrik Kampnagel ein aufregendes Programm, das von zeitgenössischen Theater-, Tanz- und Performanceveranstaltungen über Konferenzen zu politischen und gesellschaftstheoretischen Themen bis zu erlesenen Popkonzerten und queeren Karaokeabenden reicht. Um über dieses Programm unterhaltsam informiert zu werden, unbedingt den lässig formulierten Newsletter abonnieren.

The "Center for More Beautiful Arts" in the vast halls of the former Kampnagel factory offers an exciting program ranging from contemporary theater, dance and performance events to talks on sociology theory to A-list pop concerts and queer karaoke nights. Make sure to sign up for the Kampnagel's hip, punchy newsletter to stay on top of their entertaining schedule. **kampnagel.de**

Schachspielen im Stadtpark
Beim Lesecafé, 22303 Barmbek

Gar nicht so leicht, auf den verwitterten Stein-
platten inmitten von Bauern, Damen und Kö-
nigen den Überblick zu behalten. Eine echte
sportliche Herausforderung ist das Bodenschach außerdem, denn
die kniehohen Figuren wollen bewegt werden, und das, während
die Zuschauer auf den Picknickbänken drumherum jeden Zug kom-
mentieren. Von der Anstrengung ermattet, erholen sich die Spieler
anschließend nebenan im Lesecafé.

*Sometimes it's hard to get an overview out here on the
weathered stone slabs surrounded by pawns, queens and kings.
Ground chess is also a real athletic challenge because you need to
push around those knee-high pieces while the audience on the picnic benches second-guesses your every move. Exhausted from their
efforts, players can retire next door to recoup at the Lesecafé.*

Trinkhalle
Südring 1, 22303 Barmbek

Beim Wort Trinkhalle denkt man nicht gerade
an stilvoll-schlichtes Ambiente mit Parkblick
und guten, starken Kaffee, sondern an einen
verlotterten Kiosk für das Nötigste — den Alkohol. Das Café Trinkhalle heißt allerdings nicht so, weil es einer heutigen Trinkhalle äh-
nelt, sondern weil es sich in dem alten Klinkergebäude im Stadtpark
befindet, das vor hundert Jahren als Ausschankhalle für Heilwasser
gebaut wurde.

*A Trinkhalle is normally a kiosk selling booze, cigarettes
and other necessities of daily life—but this one is a stylish café and
beer garden offering views of the Stadtpark and good strong coffee.
Its name derives from the brick building, constructed almost a century ago, that originally dispensed mineral water to thirsty, health-
conscious customers.* **trinkhalle-hamburg.de**

138

Das hat an dieser ruhigen Kreuzung einer Barmbeker Seitenstraße wirklich noch gefehlt: Nóra Horváths Bistro mit ausgewählten Gerichten aus saisonalen Zutaten (von Nicht-Vegetariern hört man, das Pulled Pork sei hervorragend). Im Winter sitzt man im runden Schaufenster des denkmalgeschützten Klinkerbaus in der Sonne und im Sommer an den Tischen davor.

This quiet intersection on a side street in Barmbek was really missing something before Nóra Horváth opened her bistro, with select dishes made with seasonal ingredients (non-vegetarians say the pulled pork is outstanding). In winter guests sit in the sunny, round showcase window of the listed brick building and in summer at the tables out front. spajz.de

139

Toll! Ein ganzer Raum voller Buchstaben! Welches beseelte Wesen würde da nicht Schnappatmung bekommen? Als Yves und Sabine Freundt 2004 anfingen, mit den Buchstaben alter Ladenschilder zu handeln, hat zwar noch niemand daran gedacht, sich Vintage-Neon übers Bett zu hängen, aber inzwischen kaufen selbst große Versandhäuser ihre typografischen Dekoelemente bei Freundts. Wenn man einen Termin vereinbart, darf man auch mal im Lager ihres Onlineshops stöbern. Dabei aber bitte immer schön weiteratmen.

If you think words are beautiful, you'll love this entire room full of letters of the alphabet. Yves and Sabine Freundt began dealing in letters from old shop signs in 2004, and today they sell both to individuals and large companies. Their vintage neon creations are particularly popular, and while the shop is online, you can poke around in their stockroom by appointment. freundts.de

HOHE EIMSBÜTTEL LUFT

Gorilla Grill
Eppendorfer Weg 58, 20259 Eimsbüttel

Der große Raum wirkt zuerst ein bisschen wie eine Kantine, denn es hallt laut zwischen dem schicken Terrazzoboden und den Stahlträgern, und die Tische stehen dicht an dicht. Die Portionen sind ordentlich, aber da hören die Ähnlichkeiten mit einer Kantine auch schon auf, denn das Essen im Gorilla Grill ist sehr gut und ebenso eigenwillig geschmackvoll wie die Einrichtung.

At first the spacious dining room feels a bit like a cafeteria—sounds reverberate loudly between the chic terrazzo flooring and supporting steel beams, and the tables are close together. The portions are ample, too, but that's where the similarities to a canteen end, because the food at the Gorilla Grill is awfully good—and just as unconventionally tasteful as the interior design. **gorilla-grill.de**

Café Osterdeich
Müggenkampstraße 34, 20257 Eimsbüttel

Auf der Suche nach einem gemütlichen Café in Eimsbüttel lohnt es sich, die belebte und an Cafés nicht eben arme Osterstraße noch ein Stückchen weiter hochzulaufen. Dorthin, wo sie gar nicht mehr Osterstraße heißt, sondern Müggenkampstraße, bis zum Café Osterdeich. Denn die Atmosphäre in dem kleinen Café ist besonders familiär, und Kaffee, Kuchen und Frühstück sind besonders lecker.

If you are looking for a cozy café in Eimsbüttel, it pays to keep walking a bit further up busy Osterstrasse, itself not exactly wanting for cafés, to where the name changes from Osterstrasse to Müggenkampstrasse, where you will find Café Osterdeich. The atmosphere of this small café has a real informal feel, and the coffee, cakes and breakfasts are all extra-yummy. **osterdeich.net**

142

Müggenkampstraße 43, 20257 Eimsbüttel

Eigentlich gibt es im Filmraum nur drei Abteilungen: die Abteilung Oh-den-kenn-ich-der-ist-super, die Abteilung Ach-den-wollte-ich-schon-immer-mal-sehen und die Abteilung Ah-das-sieht-ja-spannend-aus-kenn-ich-gar-nicht. Die Auswahl an Autoren- und Programmfilmen ist exquisit, und es leuchtet sofort ein, dass der Filmraum die Bezeichnung „Filmothek" im Untertitel führt — „Videothek" wäre einfach zu schnöde.

Actually, Filmraum only has three sections: the Ah-I-Know-That-One-It's-Great section; the Oh-I-Always-Wanted-To-See-That-One section; and the Hmmm-That-Looks-Interesting-I've-Never-Seen-That-One section. The selection of auteur and art house films is superb. You immediately get why Filmraum bills itself as a Filmothek. Video store would be just too ordinary. filmraum.net

143

Café Mexico

Weidenallee 6, 20357 Eimsbüttel

Eins gleich vorweg: Den Service im Café Mexico sollte man nicht an deutschen Maßstäben messen. Aber vielleicht ist der Service ja nur genauso „authentisch" wie das Essen, denn das ist unzweifelhaft super, und wenn man in puncto Service gelassen bleibt, kann man es umso mehr genießen. Dazu gibt es eine Auswahl von über einhundert Sorten Tequila, und — äußerst selten in Hamburg — die süße mexikanische Reismilch-Horchata.

One thing for starts: do not judge the service in the Café Mexico by German standards. Then again, maybe the service is just as "authentic" as the food, which is absolutely great. And if you adopt a relaxed attitude, you can enjoy it all the more. There is also a selection of over one hundred varieties of tequila, plus the sweet Mexican rice milk Horchata, a real rarity in Hamburg. cafemexico.de

Ökö-Markt in Eppendorf

Aufstieg:

Eimsbüttel
Bezirksamt
SPD-Haus eidS
rei

Ecke Bismarckstr.
Hoheluftbr.
Morgetha-Cafe

Mit Bus 5 zum Hbf

Ausstieg

Hamburg:

www.Warenwirtschaft.de

Bio-Laden
+ Cafe

Wasserschloss
Speicherstadt
(Teekontor)
Dienerreihe 4
Speicherstadt
Kaffeerösterei Speicher-
stadt
Kehrwieder 5

Alles unverpackt:
St. Pauli Twelve Monkeys
+ veganer Laden
Eimsbüttel: Bio.lose - Laden

Jimmy Elsass
Schäferstraße 26, 20357 Eimsbüttel

Bei Jimmy Elsass gibt es sehr, sehr, sehr gute Flammkuchen. Die sind nicht ganz billig, dafür sind im Preis inbegriffen: gute Musik, entspannter Service, Fotoalbum-Speisekarten mit Reisesouvenirs, riesige Weinreben als Deckenlampen, laue Abende draußen oder schummrige Abende drinnen – und natürlich ausgesprochen gute Flammkuchen.

Jimmy Elsass serves up very, very, very tasty Alsatian Flammkuchen (tarte flambée). They don't come cheap, but the price also includes: good music, laid-back service, menus with photo album that double as travel souvenirs, huge grape vines as ceiling lamps, balmy evenings outdoors or cozy evenings inside—and of course one delicious Flammkuchen. jimmyelsass.de

LIV
Lutterothstraße 8, 20255 Eimsbüttel

Eigentlich wollte Mareike Reimers nur junges deutsches und skandinavisches Design führen. Aber dann hat sie sich gegen die strenge Auswahl entschieden, und das passt zu der freundlichen Atmosphäre ihres Ladens, wo spielerischer Minimalismus mit Vorliebe für illustrative Dekors und figürliche Gestaltung regiert. Eigene Papeterie, leuchtende Regenjacken und feingliedrige Stringregale machen einen schönen Mix – nicht alles aus dem hohen Norden, aber sehr skandinavisch im Geiste.

Actually Mareike Münder only wanted to have young German and Scandinavian designers in her range. But then she decided against such strict rules, which matches the friendly atmosphere of her shop. Here reigns a playful minimalism and obvious love of illustrated prints and figurative design. Her own stationary line, bright rain jackets and delicate string shelves make for a nice mix—and not all from way up north, but very Scandinavian in spirit. livhamburg.de

Auf den ersten Blick wirkt das Geschirr in Susanne Behrens' Ladenwerkstatt schlicht und klassisch. Doch bei genauerem Hinsehen zeigt sich, dass die Keramikerin nicht nur handwerklich, sondern künstlerisch arbeitet. Noch bei der einfachsten Tasse verbindet sie Inspirationen von Pflanzen und Meer mit der Lust am Experimentieren mit Formen und Glasuren. Dass jedes Stück ein Unikat ist, versteht sich von selbst.

At first glance, the dishes in Susanne Behrens' studio-cum-store look simple and classic. But a closer look at her work reveals that the ceramist's artistic skill matches her technical skill. Even her most basic cups combine plant and nautical inspirations with a love of experimentation with shapes and glazes. Clearly, every piece is an only-of-its-kind original. **susannebehrens.de**

Was das Bier angeht, war lange alles klar: Hopfen und Malz, Gott erhalt's. Doch seit einigen Jahren gibt es handwerklich gebrautes Craft Beer und mit ihm die Vorurteile gegen das neue Brauwesen. Puristen schmeckt das gar nicht, aber alle anderen können im Taproom von Beyond Beer 300 Sorten Flaschenbier und verschiedene Fassbiere probieren und zur Krönung in Workshops lernen, ihr eigenes Bierchen zu brauen.

As far as beer goes, the mandate had always been crystal-clear: Hopfen und Malz, Gott erhalt's—God save hops and malt! But artisanally brewed craft beers have been on the rise in recent years, and the trend has gone hand-in-hand with a rise in prejudice against this new brewing method. Purists' tastes notwithstanding, everyone else can enjoy 300 varieties of bottled beer and numerous draft beers in Beyond Beer's taproom, and can top it all off by learning in workshops how to brew their own beer. **beyondbeer.de**

Interiör – Design im Viertel
Osterstraße 164, 20255 Eimsbüttel

„Design im Viertel" — das Viertel sind die Wohnstraßen rund um die Osterstraße, und nirgends wäre dieser Laden mit seinen geradlinigen Designs richtiger als im unaufgeregten Eimsbüttel. Im Sortiment dominieren schlichtes Porzellan, Küchenutensilien in knalligen Farben, schöne Stoffe und clevere Lichtutensilien — das meiste von dänischen Herstellern und alles so formschön wie praktisch: Warum Geschenkkäufer hier wohl öfter das gleiche Teil zweimal zur Kasse tragen?

"Design in the neighborhood"—the neighborhood means the residential streets around Osterstrasse. And nowhere would this shop with its linear design be more at home than in the relaxed neighborhood of Eimsbüttel. The store features simple ceramics, kitchen utensils in bright colors, beautiful fabrics and clever light fixtures. All of it is both beautiful and practical, most coming from Danish manufacturers. It's no wonder that people shopping for gifts often buy two of the same item here. **interioer.de**

Der Stuhl
Eppendorfer Weg 2, 20259 Eimsbüttel

Wer Design-Klassiker restauriert und verkauft, braucht sich um seine Schaufensterdekoration nicht andauernd Gedanken zu machen. Ein Schaukelstuhl, eine Garderobe und eine Kinderwiege aus Bugholz — die Ausstellungsstücke im Verkaufsraum dieses ganz auf Thonet-Möbel rund um den berühmten Kaffeehausstuhl spezialisierten Ladens wechseln nur selten. Das Glück, das in solcher Beschränkung liegen muss, vermittelt die ruhige Werkstattatmosphäre, in der sich die beiden Inhaber auf ihr Handwerk konzentrieren und ihre Kunden freundlich beraten.

If you're in the business of restoring and selling iconic designs, you don't need to worry too much about your store window display. A rocking chair, a wardrobe, a bentwood cradle: the items on display in the showroom of this store dedicated entirely to Thonet furniture and the famous Vienna bentwood café chair rarely change. The joy that must lie in such a narrow specialization is evoked by the quiet workshop atmosphere, in which the two owners focus on their craft and offer friendly advice to their customers.
der-stuhl-hamburg.de

150

Frau Hansen
Osterstraße 170, 20255 Eimsbüttel
Das Konzept dieses Stores ist einfach: Nicole Hansen kuratiert konsequent nur die Kleidung, Designobjekte und Möbel, die sie selbst auch tragen, verwenden oder in ihre Wohnung stellen würde. Frau Hansens treffsicher guten Geschmack bringt ihr Slogan „Wo die schönen Dinge wohnen" genau auf den Punkt.

The store concept is simple: Nicole Hansen consistently curates exclusively clothes, designer pieces and furniture that she herself would wear, use or display in her home. Ms. Hansen's unerringly good taste is summed up perfectly by her motto: "Where the finer things live." **frau-hansen.de**

151

Eclair au Café
Eppendorfer Weg 1, 20259 Eimsbüttel
Millefeuilles, Religieuse caramel, Tarte citron — wer hätte das gedacht: ein Stückchen Paris an der Ecke Eppendorfer Weg/Eimsbütteler Chaussee. Im schönen Eclair au Café mit den hohen Decken, großen Schaufenstern und gemütlicher Vintage-Einrichtung wähnt man

sich wirklich fast in einem französischen Kaffeehaus – besonders wegen der köstlichen Patisserie.

Millefeuilles, religieuse caramel, tarte citron—who would expect to find a slice of Paris at the corner of Eppendorfer Weg and Eimsbütteler Chaussee? The high ceilings, spacious front windows and cozy vintage decor of the lovely Eclair au Café really do make you think you may have wandered into a French café—don't miss out on their delectable pastries. **eclairaucafe.de**

Lys Vintage
Eppendorfer Weg 8, 20259 Eppendorf

So manche Nase wurde am Schaufenster dieses Ladens schon plattgedrückt, denn bei aller Perfektion wirkt er nicht wie ein kühl berechneter Showroom, sondern immer einladend. Lys Vintage startete vor einigen Jahren mit skandinavischen Design-Klassikern der 1950er und 1960er Jahre, mit der Zeit haben sich auch die Produkte junger nordeuropäischer Designer ins Angebot gemischt. Dass sich der Übergang von den älteren zu den allerneuesten skandinavischen Designs fast unmerklich vollzogen hat, lässt schon ahnen: Hier stehen die Klassiker von morgen.

A few noses have gotten stuck, plastered to this display window. For all its perfection, Lys Vintage is not an off-putting, slick showroom but rather an inviting store. It started out several years ago with Scandinavian design classics from the 1950s and 1960s and gradually brought in the work of young northern European designers. The nearly invisible transition from early Scandinavian design to avant-garde is a sure sign you'll find things here that will always remain timeless classics. **lys-vintage.com**

153

Lappenbergsallee 48, 20257 Eimsbüttel

Das portugiesische Café Transmontana bietet den Milchkaffee namens Galão an, aber es kann nichts für die Entwicklung, an deren Ende der Platz vor der Roten Flora „Piazza" hieß und der Abschnitt zwischen Susannenstraße und Rosenhofstraße „Galãostrich". Das Transmontana II ist die weniger überlaufene Schwester der portugiesischen Pastelaria und bietet die gleichen Köstlichkeiten — Stichwort: Nata.

This Portuguese pastelaria—the less crowded sister of the Transmontana on Schulterblatt street—is much more than just a perfect place to enjoy a galão coffee. Just try their delicious pastéis de nata egg tart pastries and you'll understand why!

154

Karussell
Fruchtallee 114, 20259 Eimsbüttel

Eine Szene-Kneipe an der Fruchtallee aufmachen? Schlau, sehr schlau, denn wie die Frau am Nebentisch schon sagt: „Ich fahr hier jeden Tag mit dem Fahrrad vorbei." Genau, und wenn man fünfmal am Karussell vorbeigefahren ist, will man selbst auch mal mit Bier oder Kaffee vor dem kleinen Souterrainladen in der Sonne sitzen und der Musik der vierspurigen Straße zuhören. Drinnen am Tresen kann man die Hände in Kronenkorken baden, sie werden dort in einer Art Trog gesammelt und zeigen an, wie beliebt die Wohnzimmeratmosphäre des winzigen Ladens ist.

Open a hipster pub on the Fruchtallee? Clever, very clever, because as the woman at the next table says: "I ride past here every day on my bike." Exactly, and once you've gone by the Karussell a few times yourself, you'll also want to drink a coffee or a beer out in the sun in front of the small basement café and listen to the music of the busy four-lane street. Inside at the bar, you can dip your hands in the

*trough full of bottle caps, proof of just how much everyone loves this
tiny place with the living-room atmosphere.* **wie-ein-karussell.de**

Motel Hamburg
Hoheluftchaussee 117–119, 20253 Hoheluft

Die „sehr guten Parkmöglichkeiten", mit denen
das Motel Hamburg lockt, sind kein leeres Ver-
sprechen, denn hier parkt man sein Auto in der
Garage direkt unterm Bett. Für Automobilisten, die es praktisch
mögen oder unter Trennungsangst von ihrem Gefährt leiden, ist die
denkmalgeschützte Herberge ideal, aber auch alle Fans der Fifties
werden vor den stilechten Mosaikfassaden und angesichts der Ge-
ranientöpfe vor jeder Schlafbox ins Schwelgen geraten.

*Motel Hamburg promises guests "excellent parking op-
tions" and delivers on that promise, because you can park your car
in the garage directly under your bed. While the motel, listed as a
place of historical interest, is ideal for motorists who prioritize con-
venience or who suffer from separation anxiety when too far from
their vehicle, its vintage mosaic-pattern wallpaper and flower boxes
with geraniums in front of every room make it a favorite of Fifties
buffs, too.* **motel-hamburg.de**

ALLZU NAH

175
HALBMONDSWEG
ELBTUNNEL
BERNADOTTESTRASSE
PHILOSOPHENWEG
HOHENZOLLERNRING
ELBCHAUSSEE
ELBCHAUSSEE
ÖVELGÖNNE
183
168
172

156

Eine ehrwürdige Eckkneipe mit dunkler Wandvertäfelung und großen Fenstern bekommt
einen prächtigen neuen Tresen, dazu wird eine kleine Bühne bespielt — fertig ist die Mischung aus Nachbarschaftstreff und entspannter Szenekneipe, und zwar in einem Wohnviertel, weitab vom
Schuss. Die Kneipiers arbeiten hauptberuflich im Musikbusiness,
daher das sehr gute Programm, und das Künstlerhaus Frappant ist
gleich um die Ecke.

*A venerable local pub with dark wooden paneling and
big windows gets a gorgeous new bar and a small stage—that's the
recipe for this neighborhood meeting spot-cum-trendy yet relaxed
watering hole located in a residential area well off the beaten track.
The guys who run the place have fulltime jobs in the music business,
hence the excellent calendar of live events; plus, the artists network
and exhibition space Frappant is just around the corner.* **aalhaus.de**

157

An „Damensauna"-Tagen treffen sich in der Fest-
land-Sauna nachmittags größere Gruppen lebhaf-
ter Saunafreundinnen, und abends verwandelt
sich die schöne, weitläufige Saunalandschaft in einen inoffiziellen
Lesbentreff. Im Winter teilen sich bei den stündlichen Aufgüssen
manchmal mehr als vierzig Frauen die Bänke in der 95°C Sauna, um
sich anschließend auf der Außenterrasse abzukühlen, im Whirlpool
zu entspannen oder im Ruheraum einzunicken.

*The afternoon clientele on "Ladies Sauna" days at the
Festland sauna and swim club is comprised of groups of voluble
friends, while in the evening the lovely and spacious sauna land-
scape serves as an unofficial hotspot for lesbians. In the winter*

months, sometimes 40 women and more share the sauna benches for the hourly ladling of aromatherapy water onto the rocks in the 95°C box before cooling off outside in the patio jacuzzi or dozing on a chaise longue in the quiet zone. **baederland.de**

Kühne Lage
Schützenstraße 39, 22761 Bahrenfeld

Eine ziemlich kühne Lage haben sich Dietmar Bruns und Antje Knechten für ihr sympathisches Weinbistro ausgesucht! Am Bahrenfelder Ende der Schützenstraße, im gastronomischen Niemandsland gegenüber der ehemaligen Kühne-Fabrik bieten sie eine große Auswahl guter Gewächse, die sie selbst importieren und ihrer Kundschaft nach deren individuellem Geschmack ans Herz legen. Von guter Bistrokost begleitet darf der Wein hier die Hauptrolle spielen und verwandelt die heiter-gelassene zuweilen in eine beschwingte Atmosphäre.

Dietmar Bruns and Antje Knechten chose a "bold location" for their pleasant wine bistro Kühne Lage! At the Bahrenfeld end of Schützenstrasse in the middle of a culinary no man's land across the street from the former Kühne mustard factory, they offer a wide selection of fine vintages, which they import themselves and recommend to their customers according to individual taste. Accompanied by solid bistro fare, the wine is the star of the show here, occasionally transforming the upbeat and relaxed atmosphere into a lively one. **kuehne-lage.de**

Heimat
Grosse Brunnenstraße 70, 22763 Ottensen

Für Kostümdesignerinnen wie Suscha Vogel-Lobeck gehört das Sammeln von besonderen Dingen zum Beruf. Ihre Requisiten fanden vor ein paar Jahren in einem kleinen Laden in Ottensen eine neue Heimat, nach und nach hat sie den Fundus um lauter liebenswerten Tüdelkram erweitert: regionales Kunsthandwerk und Hamburg-Accessoires, Hüte und Stulpen, Collagen in Streichholzschachteln und und und. Zu jedem Stück kann die Inhaberin eine Geschichte erzählen, das Stöbern in der Heimat — außerhalb der Öffnungszeiten auch nach telefonischer Vereinbarung: 0162 21900980 — ist deshalb immer ein Erlebnis.

For costume designers like Suscha Vogel-Lobeck, collecting special things is part and parcel of the job. A few years ago, her stage props found a new home in a small shop in Ottensen. Little by little, the inventory has been expanded to include adorable curios and knickknacks: local arts and crafts and Hamburg-themed accessories, hats and buttons, collages in matchboxes and so on. There's a story behind every item in the store and the owner will be glad to tell you about it, which makes poking around Heimat a real treat time and again.

Zur Traube
Karl-Theodor-Straße 4, 22765 Altona

160

1889 als Weinhandlung gegründet, ist Zur Traube heute Hamburgs älteste Weinstube — ein uriger Ort, der sich mit seiner großen, gläsernen Trauben-Leuchte über der Eingangstür schon von weitem als Weinlokal zu erkennen gibt. Im Winter lassen sich die exzellente Auswahl an Weinen und die französisch inspirierte Küche gemütlich drinnen im dunklen Holzdekor genießen, im Sommer auch an den Tischen draußen.

Founded in 1889 as a wine trader, today Zur Traube is Hamburg's oldest wine tavern—located in a rustically quaint building, a large glass lamp shaped like a bunch of grapes hanging over the entrance hints at the enoteca inside. In winter the outstanding selection of wines and French-inspired cuisine can be enjoyed in the cozy, dark wooden interior, while in summer guests can also dine at one of the outside tables. zur-traube.de

Kleinmöbellager
Stresemannstraße 136, 22767 Altona

Es lohnt sich, regelmäßig im Kleinmöbellager vorbei-
zuschauen. Der Arbeitskreis Lokale Ökonomie sammelt
dort Möbel, die für den Müll zu schade sind, und gibt
sie gegen eine Spende wieder ab. Lampen, Stühle, Regale, Jalousien,
aber auch ein großes Sortiment an Schrauben und anderen
Eisenwaren-Kleinteilen — der kleine Raum ist vollgestopft mit allem, was nicht gerade eine Schrankwand ist, und es gibt immer
wieder richtige Schätzchen.

*It's worth taking a peek inside this used furniture store
every now and then. Run by a group of local economic activists called
the Arbeitskreis Lokale Ökonomie, the storefront is a repository for
furniture items that are just too good for the trash. The small space
is crammed full of lamps, chairs, shelves, blinds—and hardware bits
and bobs, including a wide selection of screws and other small parts.
Pretty much everything can be found here except for huge wall units
and wardrobes, and often there are some real treasures to be had for
a small donation to cover costs.* **ak-loek.de**

Altonas Balkon
Palmaille, 22767 Altona

Maritime Biergartenatmosphäre: Auf Altonas
Balkon, der etwas versteckt in den Grünan-
lagen unterhalb der Palmaille liegt und nicht
mit dem „Altonaer Balkon" verwechselt wer-
den darf, ist das kein Widerspruch. Statt dauernd nach dem Kellner
zu sehen, schauen die Gäste entspannt auf Köhlbrandmündung
und Hafen, denn die Getränke holen sie sich am Tresen selbst. Aber
Achtung: Das kulinarische Angebot beschränkt sich auf einfache
Speisen, und an kalten und regnerischen Tagen macht der Biergarten schon um 18 Uhr zu.

A beer garden with a nautical feel: at Altonas Balkon, somewhat hidden among the landscaped green areas between Palmaille and the river and not to be confused with the nearby "Altonaer Balkon", guests can enjoy the best of both worlds. Instead of constantly looking out for their server, they can relax and enjoy the view of the Köhlbrand Bridge and the port after getting their drinks from the bar inside. But beware: The food menu is limited to snacks, and the beer garden closes at 6 p.m. on cold or rainy days.
altonas-balkon.de

163

Hafenbahnhof
Große Elbstraße 276, 22767 Altona

Der Blick auf die Elbe ist inzwischen zugebaut, aber die eigentliche Perle liegt hinter der architektonischen „Perlenkette an der Elbe" in einem ehemaligen Stationshaus der Hamburger Hafenbahn. Der Hafenbahnhof, ein kleiner geduckter Rotklinkerbau, ist Club und Café mit ungekünsteltem Publikum und gutem Programm: Konzerte, Parties, Lesungen, montags Jazz und sonntags hausgemachte Kuchen.

Thanks to urban development, the former harbor railway station no longer has a view of the Elbe, but this single-story brick building is still an architectural jewel: a café, bar and performance venue all under one roof. Don't miss the homemade cakes on Sundays and the Monday jazz sessions. **hafenbahnhof.com**

164

Jö Makrönchen
Friedensallee 6, 22765 Altona

Boah, sind die süüüüß! Die Rede ist hier nicht von Tierbabies, sondern von kleinen, bunten Köstlichkeiten aus Mandelbaiser und cremiger Ganache — Makronen. Besonders süß sind die Makronen, die es im Ladencafé von Jö Makrönchen gibt, denn der Name ist

Programm: „Jö" ist das schweizerdeutsche Wort für süß. „Makrönchen" muss wohl das schweizerdeutsche Wort für superlecker sein.

Oh, they're so sweeet! No, not baby animals, but the small, colorful delicacies made of almond meringue and creamy ganache known as macarons. The macarons at the storefront café Jö Makrönchen are very sweet indeed, as the name says it all: "Jö" is Swiss German for "sweet." "Makrönchen" must be the Swiss German word for mega-delicious then. **joe-makroenchen.de**

Frau Tulpe
Große Bergstraße 213, 22767 Altona

Dass Frau Tulpe Stoffe liebt, glaubt man ihr sofort. Ihr Laden ist ein wahres Wunderland aus bunt gemusterten Baumwollstoffen, Borten und Bändern mit modischen zeitgenössischen und klassischen, zeitlosen Designs. Dazu gibt es eine große Auswahl an allem, was man außer Stoff zum Nähen so braucht.

It is immediately apparent upon entering Frau Tulpe that the owner loves fabrics. The store is a veritable wonderland of brightly patterned cotton fabrics, trims and ribbons in trendy contemporary and classic, timeless designs. There is also a wide selection of notions for all your sewing needs beyond fabric. **frau-tulpe.de**

Eisliebe
Bei der Reitbahn 2, 22763 Ottensen

Die Eisliebe hat *wirklich* das beste Eis Hamburgs. Das beweist die Tatsache, dass die Schlange vor dem kleinen Laden in Ottensen immer mindestens drei Häuser weit reicht. Am Schaufenster klebt sogar ein Zettel mit einer Anstellanweisung: Bitte nach links anstellen, Fußgänger durchlassen, keine Hauseingänge blockieren, Fahrräder und Kinderwagen am Straßenrand abstellen. Auch wenn das Schlangestehen abschreckend klingt: Es lohnt sich, vor allem für Zimt-Pflaume.

Eisliebe truly boasts the best ice cream in town. Hamburgers know that, which is why the line out front of the narrow storefront in Ottensen invariably stretches for three buildings or more. The sidewalk gets so crowded that the store owners felt compelled to put a note in the window advising people how to act: queue to the left, let pedestrians pass, don't block building entrances, and park your bicycles and strollers on the street, please. But don't let that put you off making the trip—especially for the cinnamon plum.

Konus

Bahrenfelder Straße 59, 22765 Ottensen

Was man im Laden sieht: Designermöbel für drinnen und draußen, klassische Metallmöbel der Firma Müller und jede Menge Wohnzutaten wie die magnetischen Schlüsselbretter aus alten Verkehrsschildern. Was man nicht sieht: dass hinten in der Werkstatt neue Ideen Form bekommen und aus einer breiten Palette von Hölzern Möbel nach Maß und den Wünschen der Kunden entstehen. Eine ideale Kombination.

What you will see is a cornucopia of designer furniture for indoors and outdoors, including classic metal pieces by Müller, and home accessories like magnetic key holders made from old traffic signs. What you won't see is the behind-the-scenes workshop, where staff design and build wooden furniture to order. konus-wohnen.de

Strandperle

Övelgönne 60, 22605 Othmarschen

Die Strandperle war schon eine Strandbar, lange bevor jemand auf die Idee kam, auch dort, wo es kein Wasser gibt, Sand aufzuschütten, Schirme, Liegestühle, Palmen und eine Bar aufzustellen und das Ganze Beachclub zu nennen. Bei schönem Wetter tritt man sich rund um die Strandperle die Ohren ab, aber dafür hat man echten Elb-sand zwischen den Zehen, ein Getränk in der Hand und den Logen-platz zum Schiffebeobachten.

The Strandperle was a beach bar legend long before someone had the brainwave of dumping a bunch of sand where there is no water, setting up umbrellas, deck chairs, palm trees and a bar, and calling the whole kit and caboodle a "beach club." When the weather's fine, the beach out front gets pretty packed, but it's a fair tradeoff for the bonus of feeling genuine Elbe sand between your toes as you enjoy a front-row view of the activity on the water, beverage in hand. strandperle-hamburg.de

Altonaer Museum
Museumstraße 23, 22765 Altona

Man täusche sich nicht: Das Altonaer Museum ist nicht nur kulturhistorisches Regionalmuse-um, sondern setzt mit seinem Kinderbuchhaus, einer Dioramensammlung und der optischen Wunderkammer auf visuelle Faszination. Der Museumsshop ist selbst ein Wunderkabi-nett: Thaumatrope, Polyoramen, Um-die-Ecke-Gucker, Popup- und Flip-Books laden ein zur spielerischen Selbsttäuschung.

Make no mistake: the Altonaer Museum is more than just a museum of regional cultural history. With its "children's book house," diorama collection and chamber of optical illusions, it is also a tribute to visual wonders. The museum shop is itself an optical imaginarium, with Victorian thaumatropes, polyorama panoptiques, round-the-corner gazers, pop-ups and flip books all inviting you to explore the world of optical self-deception. altonaer-museum.de

Entwurf-Direkt
Eulenstraße 81, 22763 Ottensen

Auf den ersten Blick ist Entwurf-Direkt ein Laden für Unikatmöbel aus ausrangierten Schubladen und auf den zweiten ein Geschäft für menschenfreundliche Gebrauchskunst. Aber eigentlich ist die „Kunstkrämerei" eine soziale Plastik, denn Inhaber Per Schumann nutzt Handwerk und Kunst, um Menschen zusammenzubringen. Am liebsten bei einem großen Topf Suppe auf dem Tisch in der Mitte seines Ladens, dessen Platte im früheren Leben als Boden eines Güterwaggons durchs Land rollte.

At first glance, Entwurf-Direkt looks like a shop for one-of-a-kind furniture made from discarded drawers, and on second glance it looks like a shop for people-friendly utilitarian art. But actually this art shop is conceived of as a kind of social putty to build community, as owner Per Schumann uses craftsmanship and art to bring people together. Preferably over a big pot of soup in the middle of his store, on a table with a top that once did duty as the floor of a freight car. **entwurf-direkt.de**

Papier + Design
Bahrenfelder Straße 71, 22765 Ottensen

Dass sich in diesem wunderbaren Fachgeschäft sowohl der tägliche als auch der gehobene Bedarf an Schreibgerät, Papier und Büromaterial decken lässt, ist die Pflicht. Die Kür ist, dass die Inhaberin auf internationalen Messen Papierlampen aus Nepal, japanisches Papierklebeband, orientalische Schmuckumschläge und feine Lederwaren zusammenträgt. Und ihren Höhepunkt hat diese Kür jedes Jahr in der Vorweihnachtszeit, wenn dicke Baumkugeln und neuester Christbaumkitsch um die Aufmerksamkeit der weihnachtsseligen Ottenser buhlen.

This wonderful stationer carries everything one could need in terms of normal office supplies, plus fine writing instruments, paper and other special items. What sets this store apart though are real finds like paper lamps from Nepal, Japanese paper tape, decorative envelopes from Asia and fine leather goods, which the owner brings home from international tradeshows. She outdoes herself every year during the holiday shopping season, when big baubles and the latest Christmas tree kitsch compete for the attention of Ottensen window shoppers. **christinebruhn.de**

Restaurantschiff Bergedorf
Ponton Neumühlen, 22763 Othmarschen

Bei Sonnenschein guckt man vom offenen Oberdeck des Restaurantschiffs D.E.S. Bergedorf auf die vorbeifahrenden Schiffe, und wenn es grau und nebelig ist, sitzt es sich drinnen auf den roten Sitzbänken warm und gemütlich mit einem Glühwein in der Hand. Die ehemalige Elbfähre liegt im Museumshafen vor Anker und ist nach einem langen Spaziergang am Elbstrand die beste Adresse.

When the sun is out, the view of passing ships from the open-air upper deck of the floating restaurant D.E.S. Bergedorf is great, and when skies are misty and gray, nothing beats a mug of mulled wine in the restaurant's warm and cozy interior featuring diner-style red booths. The former Elbe River ferry is permanently moored at the "Museumshafen" historic port, and is the place to go after a long walk on the beach. **kleinhuis-restaurantschiff.de**

Café El Rojito
Große Brunnenstraße 74, 22763 Ottensen

Vor dem kleinen Café El Rojito stehen die Kinderwagen manchmal wie Pferde vor dem Saloon. Denn im schönen schattigen Hinterhofgarten

können die Kinder gefahrlos spielen, während die Mütter und Väter starken, fair gehandelten Kaffee von Kooperativen in Nicaragua trinken und die köstlichen Kuchen der Biokonditorei Eichel genießen. Gerade kein Kind zur Hand? Kein Problem, vorne an die große Schaufensterfläche gelehnt, kann man nachmittags auch allein wunderbar in der Sonne braten.

Some days, the baby strollers parked out front of the small Café El Rojito are worse than horses at a Wild West saloon. That's because the kids can romp safely in the shaded backyard garden as mom and dad sip strong, fair-trade coffee from cooperatives in Nicaragua and enjoy delicious organic cakes. Childless, you say? Not a problem—singles too can sun themselves silly in the streetside seats in front of the café's large window space. **el-rojito.de**

Café Forelle
Erzbergerstraße 14, 22765 Altona

Ach soooo! Ach so, deswegen sind die Wände türkis gefliest und die Teller und Wanddeko haben die Form von Fischen: Was heute ein liebevoll durchgestaltetes Café mit Retrocharme ist, war seit den 1920er Jahren ein Fischladen. Zum Glück weisen darauf nur noch Name und Deko hin, nicht der Geruch — statt nach Fisch riecht es nun köstlich nach Mittagstisch, Kaffee und Kuchen.

Oh, OK, so that's why the walls are turquoise-tiled and the plates and decorations are shaped like fish! What is now a lovingly appointed café in charming retro style used to be a fishmonger's shop from the 1920s until recently. Luckily, only the name and decor are redolent of this and not the smell—instead of fish, the air is now filled with the wonderful scent of lunch fare, coffee and cake. **cafe-forelle.de**

Hagenah
Schnackenburgallee 8, 22525 Bahrenfeld

Frischfisch im Gewerbegebiet: Als das im 19. Jahrhundert gegründete Groß- und Einzelhandelsgeschäft in den 1970er Jahren vom Fischmarkt ins Altonaer Hinterland zog, hielten das viele Fischliebhaber für keine gute Idee. Heute kommen sie aus ganz Hamburg zu Hagenah nach Bahrenfeld, um an der endlos langen Fischtheke heimischen Fisch und exotisches Krusten- und Schalentier zu kaufen. Zum Betrieb gehören eine der letzten Fischräuchereien Hamburgs und ein legendärer Mittagstisch mit in Butter gebratener Scholle und Seelachsfilet „natur".

Fresh fish in the middle of a commercial district? When this fish wholesaler and retailer founded in the 19th century moved from Hamburg's Fish Market to Altona's hinterland in the 1970s, many area seafood lovers were skeptical. Today, customers from all over Hamburg make the trek to Hagenah in Bahrenfeld to buy domestic and exotic fish and shellfish at the endless fish counter. The locale features one of the last remaining fish smokehouses in Hamburg and serves up a legendary lunch. **hagenah-hamburg.de**

Hamburgs Kleinstes Kaufhaus
Bahrenfelder Straße 207, 22767 Ottensen

Jürgen Behrmann schmeißt nichts weg, er sortiert nur ein: zwei Kisten alte Reisefalter, drei Becher Stricknadeln, ein Raum voll Haushaltsgeräte und einer mit Geschirr, und der ganze Himmel hängt voller Lampen. Die Waren in den vollgestopften Räumen des kleinsten Kaufhauses Hamburgs stammen aus Haushaltsauflösungen und Entrümpelungen und sind so gut sortiert, dass man hingehen kann und sagen: „Ich brauche das und das." Und Jürgen Behrmann dirigiert: „Guck mal dahinten in der Ecke."

Jürgen Behrmann doesn't throw stuff away, he just sorts through it: two boxes of old travel brochures, three mugs of knitting needles, a room full of household appliances and another one with dishes—and the entire ceiling filled with lights. The wares jammed into in the crowded rooms of the "smallest department store in Hamburg" are sourced from estate sales and attic cleanups, and are so well organized that it's hard to leave without discovering a few things you really "need." Especially with Jürgen Behrmann suggesting that you "have a look back there in the corner."
hamburgs-kleinstes-kaufhaus.de

Stilbruch
Ruhrstraße 51, 22761 Bahrenfeld

1983 wurde der Sperrmüll in Hamburg zum letzten Mal vom Straßenrand abgeholt, seitdem muss man die Stadtreinigung zu sich nach Hause bestellen (und bezahlen). Was dann abgeholt wird, können andere hinterher in einem der beiden Stilbruch-Gebrauchtwarenkaufhäuser erstehen. Die Preise sind nicht immer günstig, aber es lassen sich doch immer wieder besondere Stücke finden, übrigens nicht nur Möbel, Haushaltswaren und Bücher, sondern auch Kleidung.

In 1983, the city of Hamburg ceased curbside collection of bulky items; ever since then, residents have had to schedule—and pay for—bulk item pickup. The stuff that gets trashed can subsequently be purchased in one of the two Stilbruch thrift store outlets. The prices are not always cheap, but the stores occasionally yield some real gems—not just furniture, household goods and books, but used clothing, too. **stilbruch.de**

Adele & Clodwig
Bahrenfelder Straße 43, 22765 Ottensen

Vorne in der Spiel- und Malecke des Cafés sind die Kleinen gut beschäftigt, während ihre Eltern

in Ruhe durch die Räume voller restaurierter Möbel, Textilien und Kulinaria streifen und dann im hintersten Zimmer heimlich Kindergeschenke kaufen: handgearbeitete Spieluhren, Stofftiere und jede Menge schöne Sachen. Das Besondere: Alles, was man sieht, steht zum Verkauf, selbst die schicken restaurierten Tische im Café kann man bei Gefallen kaufen und gleich mit nach Hause nehmen.

Leave the kids in the play area at the front of the building, and feast your eyes on rooms full of restored furniture, textiles and culinary treats. The back room is devoted to gifts for children like handmade toy clocks, fluffy animals and other goodies. And everything you see is for sale—even the stylish tables in the café are yours for the asking. **adeleundclodwig.de**

Kurt Gaden
Holstenstraße 62, 22767 Altona

Die Mitarbeiter bei Kurt Gaden haben es einfach drauf. Kein Wunder, das Familienunternehmen ist ja auch schon seit über hundert Jahren im Geschäft und schneidert bis heute in der eigenen Manufaktur Zunftkleidung auf Maß. Aber auch wenn man nicht vorhat, in absehbarer Zeit auf die Walz zu gehen, lohnt sich der Weg zu Kurt Gaden — wegen der Wolltroyer und Flanellhemden, der Fleecepullis und Dickieshosen, wegen der Carharttjacken und der Stetsonmützen.

179

The staff at Kurt Gaden know what they're doing. That's not surprising, considering the family-run operation has been dressing skilled tradesmen for more than a century, and today continues to make made-to-measure workwear in its own tailor shop. Yet even if you have no pending plans to work your way around the world as a journeyman in a fancy corduroy getup, a visit to Kurt Gaden is fun—because of all the shawl collar wool sweaters, flannel shirts, fleece pullovers and Dickies work pants, plus Carhartt jackets and Stetson hats. **kurtgaden.de**

Klappe
Am Sood 2, 22765 Ottensen

Dass der Name des Lokals kein rüder Imperativ ist, sondern eine Besonderheit des Orts beschreibt, wird einem erst klar, wenn man davorsteht: Einen Gastraum gibt es nicht, die beiden Köche reichen die Teller mit ihrem „1A-Mittagstisch" durch eine Klappe in der Wand. Um diesen zu essen, muss man dann draußen im Stehen improvisieren – und lernt dabei garantiert neue Leute kennen.

That the name of this establishment is no rude imperative—Klappe being the German word for "flap" and northern German slang for "shut your hole"—but rather describes a physical feature of the location becomes clear only when you are literally standing in front of it: there is no dining area, so the two chefs serve up their self-described "A-1 lunch" through a hole in the wall. Eating said lunch requires one to dine on the fly while standing—and is a guaranteed ice-breaker with fellow guests.

Lindli Geschenkideen
Bahrenfelder Straße 127, 22765 Ottensen

Sie quietschen und klimpern, sie blinken und zucken: Die Gimmicks und Gadgets, die Michael Lohmann in seinem Laden zusammenträgt, braucht natürlich kein Mensch. Weil die Elefantenrüssel und Hasenzähne, aufziehbaren Omas und Opas und Schreibblöcke in Salamiform aber so konsequent zweckfrei sind, provozieren sie die Kundschaft immer wieder zu spontanen Bekundungen reinster Freude.

It's clear that no person on the planet needs any of the shiny, squeaky, jingly, blinking, gimmicky gadgets and doohickeys that Michael Lohmann curates in his little store. But precisely because novelty items like elephant trunks and buckteeth, wind-up grandmas and grandpas, and salami-shaped notepads are so irredeemably useless, they never fail to elicit spontaneous giddiness.

Klippkroog
Große Bergstraße 255, 22767 Altona

In der zweiten Reihe hinter dem Trubel der Neuen Großen Bergstraße ist der Klippkroog eine Überraschung. Ist das schön hier! Drinnen edel-rustikal mit rohen Holzbohlen und Beton, draußen mit Polstern und Schirmen in der Sonne. Das ausgesuchte Essensangebot ist so lecker, dass man den Slogan „Frisch auf den Tisch" glaubt, obwohl das ja immer alle behaupten.

Nestled in its second-row seat a bit removed from the bustling Neue Grosse Bergstrasse, Klippkroog is a special treat. Boy, is it nice here! Inside, the decor is upscale rustic with unfinished wooden planks and concrete, outside there are umbrellas for shade and cushions on the seats. The food on the small menu is scrumptious enough to lend credibility to the establishment's "served fresh" promise, despite the claim being far from unique. **klippkroog.de**

Himmelsleiter
22605 Othmarschen

Die Himmelsleiter führt nicht etwa hinauf zum lieben Gott, sondern auf direktem Weg hinab an den Elbstrand. Aber dort die nackten Zehen in den Sand zu stecken fühlt sich trotzdem himmlisch an, vor allem mit einem Getränk in der Hand oder abends am Lagerfeuer. Macht man sich die Mühe, die rund hundert Stufen von unten zu erklimmen, wird man oben an der Elbchaussee mit einer grandiosen Aussicht über den Hafen belohnt.

This Himmelsleiter—"stairway to heaven"—doesn't lead to the pearly gates; it's a direct path down the hill to the Elbe. But it still feels heavenly to dig your bare toes into the sand, especially with a drink in hand or huddled around a campfire. It takes some effort to ascend the hundred or so steps from the beach, but once you get to the top, you'll be rewarded with a magnificent view of the harbor.

ANNER ELBE

Römischer Garten
Falkensteiner Ufer 45, 22587 Blankenese

Ein Stück Italien am Geesthang von Blankenese,
so jedenfalls fühlt sich der Römische Garten an.
Im Stil der italienischen Renaissance gestaltet,
gehörte der Garten früher zur Villa der Bankiersfamilie Warburg
und ist heute ein öffentlicher Park mit einem Naturtheater, das
den Amphitheatern der Antike gleicht und im Sommer bespielt
wird. Die immergrüne Girlandenhecke — dreißig Meter über der
Elbe — gibt eine atemberaubende Aussicht frei.

*The Renaissance-style garden, a little piece of Italy in the
riverside suburb of Blankenese, once belonged to a villa owned by the
Warburg banking family. It is now a public park with an outdoor
amphitheater used for performances in summer. Garlanded by an
evergreen hedge and perched thirty meters above the Elbe, it offers
breathtaking views.*

Gaststätte Fährmannssand
Fährmannssand 1, 22880 Wedel

Auf dem Deich der ehemaligen Elbinsel Fährmannssand teilt man den weiten wunderbaren Blick über Elbe und Marsch mit vielen
Schafen. Wenn der Wind dann hungrig gemacht hat, stärkt man
sich in der schlichten Gaststätte Fährmannssand mit deftiger
norddeutscher Küche und beobachtet weiter, wie sich die riesigen
Containerschiffe hinterm Deich durch die Wiesen schieben.

*On the dike of the former river island Fährmannssand,
humans share the spectacular view of Elbe and marshland with a
whole lot of sheep. When the wind has worked up your appetite, have
a rest and refuel at Fährmannssand, an unassuming locale serving
hearty northern German fare—and continue to observe the huge
container ships seemingly gliding through the meadows beyond the
dike.* **faehrmannssand.de**

186

Credenza paper & more
Blankeneser Hauptstraße 153,
22587 Blankenese

Wenn man bei Credenza mal einen Kaweko-Füller in der Hand hatte, versteht man, was Menschen auch heute noch daran reizt, Schreibkultur per Füllfederhalter und Feinstpapier zu pflegen und mit Korrespondenz der eigenen Persönlichkeit Ausdruck zu verleihen. Die Inhaberin ist gerne dabei behilflich, dazu das passende Material aus ihrem exklusiven Sortiment an Papeterie und Schreibgeräten auszuwählen.

If you've ever sat at a writing desk with a freshly filled fountain pen and a sheet of virgin white paper, you'll know that even in the age of email, a handwritten letter can be a telling expression of your personality. Credenza's friendly owner will help you to find the writing implements and stationary that are exactly right for you.
credenza-hamburg.de

187

Campingplatz Elbecamp
Falkensteiner Ufer 101, 22587 Rissen

1A-Naherholung: Nachmittags schön mit dem Fahrrad an der Elbe runterfahren, unterwegs bei einem Getränk in der Strandperle pausieren und gegen Abend auf dem naturbelassenen Elbecamp die Zelte aufschlagen. Dann beim Sonnenuntergang den großen Schiffen zugucken, am Lagerfeuer Stockbrot rösten und zwischen Büschen und Dünen quasi direkt am Elbstrand schlafen.

Top-notch recreation at your doorstep: a lovely afternoon bike ride down to the Elbe followed by a beverage break at the Strandperle, and, as evening draws night, pitching a tent in the natural surroundings of Elbecamp. Then just sit back and watch the big ships go by at sunset, bake some twist bread on a stick over a campfire, and sleep beneath the stars practically right on the beach, among bushes and dunes. **elbecamp.de**

Navi: „Wittenbergener Weg"

Stand Up Paddling auf der Elbe
Hakendamm 2, 22380 Wedel

Pfff, segeln! Segeln kann ja jeder! Stehend auf einem Surfbrett übers Wasser gleiten, ohne dabei das Gleichgewicht zu verlieren — das ist die neue Herausforderung an der Elbe. Wem der große Strom nicht geheuer ist, der kann auf der Alster oder dem Stadtparksee auch eine oder zwei Nummern kleiner anfangen und in Einführungskursen Balancehalten üben.

Pfff, sailing! Anybody can sail! But gliding over the water while standing up on a surfboard without losing your balance—that is the latest sports challenge on the Elbe. Not yet ready to brave the big river? No worries: courses for beginners teach basic balancing skills and are offered at the smaller Alster Lake and even smaller Stadtparksee. sup-co.com

Ponton Op'n Bulln
Fähranleger Blankenese, 22587 Blankenese

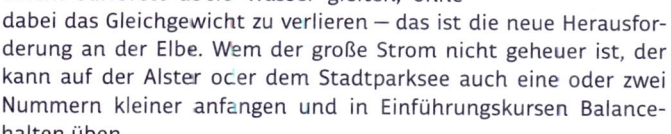

Wo sonst sollte man Fischbrötchen essen als im ehemaligen Fischerdorf Blankenese? Die schönste Kulisse dazu bietet der Ponton Op'n Bulln am Strandweg, direkt dort, wo die Fähren anlegen und die „Bergziegen" halten. Mit den Fischerhäuschen und den Elbhangvillen im Rücken sitzt man dort nicht nur am Wasser, sondern auf dem Wasser — je nach Pegel mal höher und mal tiefer.

What better place could there be to eat a fish roll than the former fishing village of Blankenese? Ponton Op'n Bulln offers the most spectacular scenery to enjoy one, right on the ferry landing where the ferries dock and the small busses—the "mountain goats"—come to rest after descending the steep slope to the Elbe. With your back to the fisherman's cottages and the villas perched high above the Elbe, you're not only sitting at the water but literally on the water—higher or lower, depending on the tide.

190

Nach vielen Stufen unten an der Elbe angekommen, kann man zum Glück den Bus nehmen, um den „Berg" wieder hinaufzukommen. Die extra kleinen Busse der HVV-Linie 48 schlängeln sich auf der Rundfahrt vom und zum S-Bahnhof Blankenese mit ihren vielsprachigen Fahrgästen durch die schmalen steilen Gassen. Und die Touristen gucken ehrfürchtig, wenn Anwohnerinnen ihren Busfahrer per Handschlag begrüßen und sich mit „Uwe, lässt' mich hinten raus?" verabschieden.

Once you finally descend all the steps to arrive at the riverfront below, your legs will appreciate being able to hop on the bus to get back up the "mountain" again. Departing from and returning to the S-Bahn station at Blankenese, the diminutive buses of the number 48 line snake along the steep and narrow lanes, filled with the polyglot sounds of their passengers. And the tourists look on with respect as local residents greet their bus driver with a handshake, and bid adieu by asking, "Hey Uwe, can you let me out the back?"

191

Wer Handel treibt, muss freundlich sein. Das wissen die Hamburger, und deshalb erbieten beim Willkomm-Höft am Schulauer Fährhaus im Westen Hamburgs fünf „Begrüßungskapitäne" den in den Hamburger Hafen einlaufenden Schiffen durch ein Flaggenritual die nötige Höflichkeit. Den größeren Schiffen erweisen sie ihr Taktgefühl sogar durch Abspielen der Nationalhymne ihres Heimatlandes und eine Begrüßung in der jeweiligen Landessprache. Und den Schaulustigen im Fährhaus erklären sie freundlicherweise die Eigenarten der begrüßten Schiffe.

Friendliness is a sine qua non for anyone engaged in trade and commerce. Hamburgers know this, which is why five "welcome captains" display the requisite politeness to ships entering the port of Hamburg with a ritual flag ceremony at Willkomm-Höft—or Welcome Point—located at Schulauer Fährhaus in the western part of the city. Larger ships are saluted by playing the national anthem of their country of origin and are welcomed in their native language. The "captains" also explain the idiosyncrasies of the ships being welcomed to the assembled onlookers in the ferry station building.
schulauer-faehrhaus.de

Lühmanns Teestube
Blankeneser Landstraße 29,
22578 Blankenese

Das muss man im Winter machen: einen ordentlichen Elbspaziergang ganz von Teufelsbrück bis Blankenese, mit letzter Kraft durchs Treppenviertel den Elbhang hoch und dann schön bei Lühmanns aufwärmen. In ihrer atmosphärischen Teestube zelebrieren die Lühmanns Genüsse englischer Art — Cream Tea, Scones und Pies — und bieten als Restaurant außerdem vegetarische Gerichte an.

In winter, take a brisk walk along the Elbe from Teufelsbrück to Blankenese, drag your cold, tired body up the steep hillside steps, and take refuge in the cozy warmth of Lühmann's. This atmospheric teahouse offers British delicacies like cream teas and pies, plus a range of vegetarian dishes. **luehmanns-teestube.de**

ÜBER

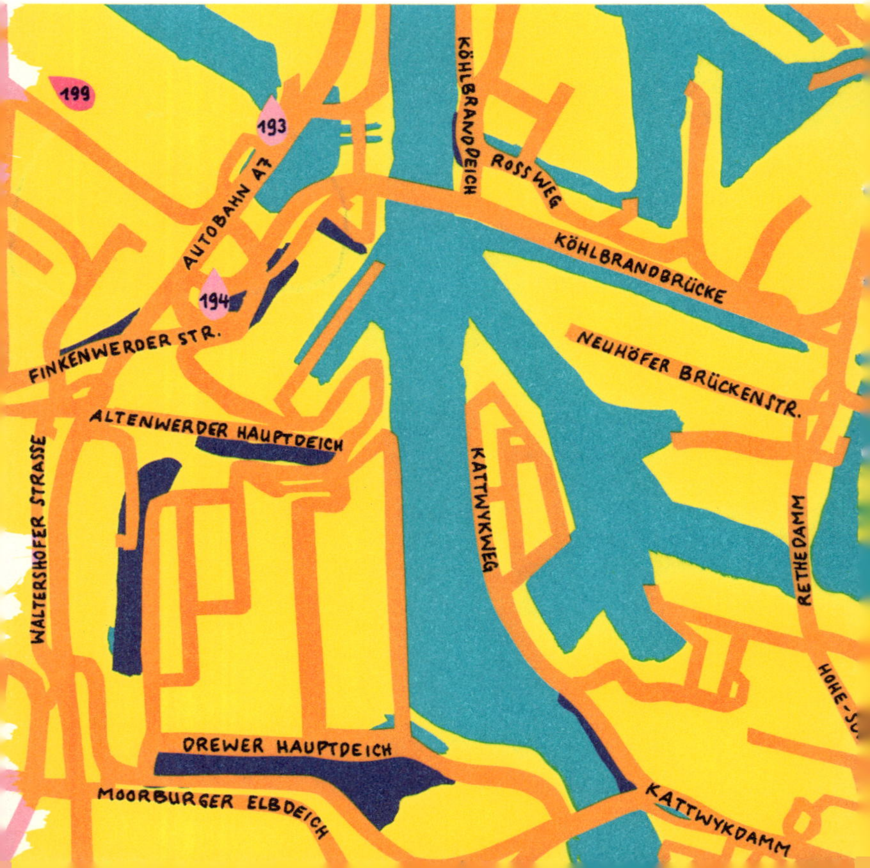

KÖHLBRANDDEICH

ROSSWEG

KÖHLBRANDBRÜCKE

NEUHÖFER BRÜCKENSTR.

AUTOBAHN A7

FINKENWERDER STR.

ALTENWERDER HAUPTDEICH

WALTERSHOFER STRASSE

KATTWYKWEG

RETHEDAMM

HOHE-SW.

DREWER HAUPTDEICH

MOORBURGER ELBDEICH

KATTWYKDAMM

199

193

194

DIE ELBE

Containerbrückenballett
Beim Fähranleger Waltershof

„Containerbrückenballett" nennen es manche. Das klingt irgendwie nach Hafenkitsch aus der Touristinfo, aber nur so lange, bis man selbst mal die Fähre nach Waltershof genommen hat, um im Schatten der Köhlbrandbrücke neben der Autobahn mitten im Industriehafen stehend über die Containerterminals zu schauen. Es sieht nämlich wirklich so aus, als würden die riesigen Hafenkräne die unzähligen bunten Container in einer geheimen Choreografie bewegen.

Some people call it "container crane ballet," and though that may sound like a line from some maritime tourist trap brochure, you'll understand why once you take the ferry to Waltershof and glance back towards the container terminals from the shadow of the Köhlbrandbrücke and the autobahn from the middle of the industrial harbor. It really does look as if the giant cranes of the port are mystically choreographed with the countless colorful cargo containers.

Über die Köhlbrandbrücke
HVV-Bushaltestelle Zollamt Waltershof
Finkenwerder Straße 4, 21129 Wilhelmsburg

Und wenn man nun schon unter der Köhlbrandbrücke durchgeschippert ist, sollte man auch gleich noch die dreieinhalb Kilometer über das Hamburger Wahrzeichen fahren. Dazu empfiehlt es sich, beim Zollamt Waltershof in den 151er Bus zu steigen, um von einem Fensterplatz auf der linken Seite die unübertroffene Aussicht auf die Stadt aus 58 Meter Höhe zu genießen — solange es noch geht, denn die schönste Brücke Europas soll irgendwann durch eine neue ersetzt werden.

Once you've passed under the Köhlbrand bridge on a boat, you should go ahead and see this Hamburg landmark from above on the 3.5-kilometer return trip. The best way to enjoy an unsurpassed view of the city from 58 meters up is to take the number 151 bus from Zollamt Waltershof and grab a window seat on the left—and be sure to hurry while you still can, because Europe's most beautiful bridge is scheduled to be replaced by a new one.

Black Ferry
Fährstraße 56, 21107 Wilhelmsburg

Seit es Black Ferry gibt, müssen die Menschen von südlich der Elbe nicht mehr nach St. Pauli übersetzen, um ihren Bedarf an veganen Lebensmitteln und Vinyl, engagierter Fachliteratur und bedruckten T-Shirts, schwarzen Kapuzenpullis und anderen Antifa-Accessoires zu decken. Ein paar Freunde haben sich als Kollektiv zusammengetan und betreiben den Laden nebenbei. Wenn's drunter und drüber geht, wird „aufgrund absoluter Verpeiltheit" auch mal früher zugemacht, aber sonst ist alles absolut super.

Ever since Black Ferry opened its doors, people from south of the Elbe no longer have to cross the river to St. Pauli to satisfy their demand for things vegan and vinyl, activist literature, silkscreen t-shirts, black hoodies, and other anti-fascist swag. A few buddies got together, formed a co-op and run the store as a side venture. When things get too crazy, they've been known to close up shop early "due to utter chaos;" but everything else about the place is absolutely great.

Café Kaffeeliebe
Fährstraße 69, 21107 Wilhelmsburg

Noch sind Cafés wie das Café Kaffeeliebe in Wilhelmsburg selten. Daran, dass sich der Stadtteil langsam verändert und sie nun auftauchen, scheiden sich die Geister, aber dann und wann wollen trotzdem alle mal einen guten Coffee-to-go und haben gegen selbstgebackenen Kuchen oder ein Päuschen auf den Polstern nichts einzuwenden.

Cafés like Café Kaffeeliebe are still few and far between in Wilhelmsburg. While opinions may differ about the district's slowly changing face as they do begin to emerge, everyone enjoys a good cup of coffee to go every now and then, and nobody has anything against a cake made from scratch or a comfy cushion ensemble. **kaffeeliebe.hamburg**

197

Selberbaggern bei Wilko Wagner
Hovestraße 31–33, 20539 Veddel

Wahrscheinlich standen so oft staunende Schaulustige vorm Bauzaun, wenn die Arbeiter von Wilko Wagner ans Werk gingen, dass so ein Nebengeschäft entstanden ist. Jedenfalls bietet die Baufirma auf der Veddel inzwischen auch „Selberbaggern" an. Ob Kettenbagger, Radlader oder Minibagger: „Unser Personal führt sie langsam und leicht verständlich in die Grundlagen des Baggerns ein." Nur erfolgreiches Angraben, das lernt man dabei nicht.

In all likelihood, the construction workers employed by Wilko Wagner elicited astonished gazes from curious onlookers beyond the fence so often that the idea for a side business was born. In any case, the construction company based in Veddel now offers lessons in DIY: dig it yourself. Customers can operate a track excavator, earthmover or mini-digger: "Our employees give you a step-by-step, easy to understand introduction to the basics of digging." The only thing they can't teach you is how to dig for gold. **baggerplatz.de**

198

Windmühle Johanna
Schönenfelder Straße 99, 21109 Wilhelmsburg

Wo heute die Windmühle „Johanna" steht, hatten im Laufe der Jahrhunderte schon vier andere Windmühlen ihren Platz. Die letzte Müllerin, die die Windmühle bis in die 1960er Jahre betrieb, hieß Johanna Sievers; dass ihre ehemalige Wirkungsstätte als instandgesetztes Denkmal nach ihr benannt und wieder in Betrieb genommen wurde, hat sie noch miterlebt. Und so wird hier für Besucher seit einigen Jahren wieder mit Windkraft gemahlen und im neuen Steinofen das begehrte „Wilhelmsburger Mühlenbrot" gebacken.

Throughout the centuries, four other windmills have been erected on the spot where today the windmill "Johanna" stands. Johanna Sievers was the last miller to operate the windmill. She retired in the late 1960s, but lived to see her former workplace recommissioned and listed as a historical monument, as well as being renamed after her. And so for some years now, the wind-powered mill has been grinding wheat, which is then baked in the new stone oven to produce the coveted "Wilhelmsburger Mühlenbrot" for visitors.
windmuehle-johanna.de

Freibad Finkenwerder
Finksweg 82, 21129 Finkenwerder

Wohl denen, die gerade auf der Leiter zur Rutsche stehen, wenn wieder ein großer Frachter herannaht, denn dort hat man die beste Aussicht über den Zipfel Land zwischen Köhlfleet und Steendiekkanal auf die Elbe. Lange schauen is aber nich, denn wie auf der Köhlbrandbrücke wird von hinten gedrängelt, und man kann kaum anhalten, um die Aussicht zu genießen. Also schnell weiter hoch und dann nach einer kurzen Rutschpartie per Arschbombe ins Becken.

It's a lucky break for people lining up on the ladder for the waterslide when a large freighter comes into view, because they have the best vantage point of the tip of land between Köhlfleet and Steendiekkanal on the Elbe. They can't linger over the beauty, though, because the great push from behind is like the traffic on the Köhlbrandbrücke. The best thing to do then is to keep moving up, take your turn on the slide, and hit the pool with a cannonball splash. **baederland.de/bad/finkenwerder.php**

Café vju im Energiebunker
Neuhöfer Straße 7, 21107 Wilhelmsburg

Die ganz große Übersicht hat man durch die Glasfront des Café vju. Von hier, von südlich der Elbe, sieht Hamburg noch mal ganz anders aus. Mit einem guten Kaffee in der Hand blickt man nach Norden auf die Stadt und kann hinterher bei einem Gang auf der „Kragplatte" des ehemaligen Flakbunkers in dreißig Metern Höhe die Aussicht in alle Richtungen bestaunen.

Hamburg looks quite different when seen through the expansive glass façade of Café vju. The "vju" from here, on the south side of the Elbe, is amazing. Enjoy a fine cup of coffee while looking north at the city skyline, and afterwards take a stroll on the cantilever walkway around the former anti-aircraft bunker and marvel at the panoramic view from thirty meters. **vju-hamburg.de**

Hamam Palace
Veringstraße 60, 21107 Wilhelmsburg

Irgendwann wird die Haut so schön schrumpelig und weich von dem heißen Dampf im Hamam. Man schrubbt ein paar Hautschichten ab und unterhält sich gut, die Muskeln lassen locker, die Sorgen fliegen davon. Das funktioniert besonders gut im Winter, denn dann ist der warme Marmorpalast mit seinem gedämpften Licht so ziemlich das Gegenteil der kaltgrauen Zumutungen draußen.

The hot steam of the hamam turns the skin wonderfully soft and pruney. Slough off a few layers of skin in a thoroughly pleasant environment, as your muscles relax and your troubles evaporate in the mist. It works wonders, especially in winter, when the warm marble palace with its subdued light is pretty much the polar opposite of the cold, gray weariness outside. **hamampalace.de**

Veddeler Fischgaststätte
Tunnelstraße 70, 20539 Veddel

Manche, die nicht mit der Zeit gehen, sind ihr irgendwann voraus. Die Einrichtung im kleinen Flachbau der Veddeler Fischgaststätte hat sich jedenfalls seit den 1950er Jahren nicht verändert, und das Angebot Fischfilet und Kartoffelsalat ist so schlicht und ergreifend, dass die Alternativen Brathering und Pommes daneben fast exotisch erscheinen. Die 37 Plätze sind *sehr* begehrt und das schon seit über 75 Jahren.

Some folks that don't move with the times somehow end up ahead of them. The decor inside the modest low-rise building occupied by the Veddeler Fischgaststätte clearly hasn't changed much since the 1950s, and the fish filet and potato salad special is so simple and compelling, it makes the competing plate of fried herring and French fries seem almost exotic. The 37 seats are an extremely hot commodity, and have been for over 75 years.

veddeler-fischgaststaette.de

Nordwandhalle
Am Inselpark 20, 21109 Wilhelmsburg

Alter, ist das anstrengend! Körperspannung ist alles beim Klettern und wenn es daran hapert, hängt man an den Griffen wie ein nasser Sack. Zum Glück kommt man in der nagelneuen Nordwandhalle leicht mit erfahreneren Kletterern ins Gespräch und kann sich Tipps geben lassen oder allein vom Zuschauen lernen, wie man über die bunten Pickel an der Wand am besten bis ganz nach oben kommt.

Dude, this is so exhausting! Climbing is all about body tension, and if you fail to master it you can end up hanging from the handholds like a wet rag. Fortunately, it's easy to meet and mingle with more experienced climbers at the brand-new Nordwandhalle and get tips or just learn by watching how best to navigate the colorful grips to the top of the wall. **nordwandhalle.de**

ALPHABET

RUBRIKEN

TOLL! DANKE!

Natali Abhyankar, Bianca Buhmann und Janni Froese
und allen, die mir Tipps für Tolle Orte gegeben haben.

IMPRESSUM

Junius Verlag GmbH
Stresemannstraße 375
22761 Hamburg
junius-verlag.de

Text, Illustration & Gestaltung: Chris Campe, allthingsletters.com
Übersetzung: Julie Niederhauser, Susan Spies, Phil Goddard
networktranslators.de
Druck und Bindung:
Textschrift: Respublika FY, der Rest ist handgezeichnet

Printed in Germany
ISBN 978-3-88506-035-2
2. Auflage 2017

Bibliografische Information der Deutschen Nationalbibliothek:
Die Deutsche Nationalbibliothek verzeichnet diese Publikation
in der Deutschen Nationalbibliografie; detaillierte bibliografische
Daten sind im Internet über http://dnb-nb.de abrufbar.